.hack

// AI buster 2

**Story by
Tatsuya Hamazaki**

**Illustrated by
Rei Idumi**

HAMBURG // LONDON // LOS ANGELES // TOKYO

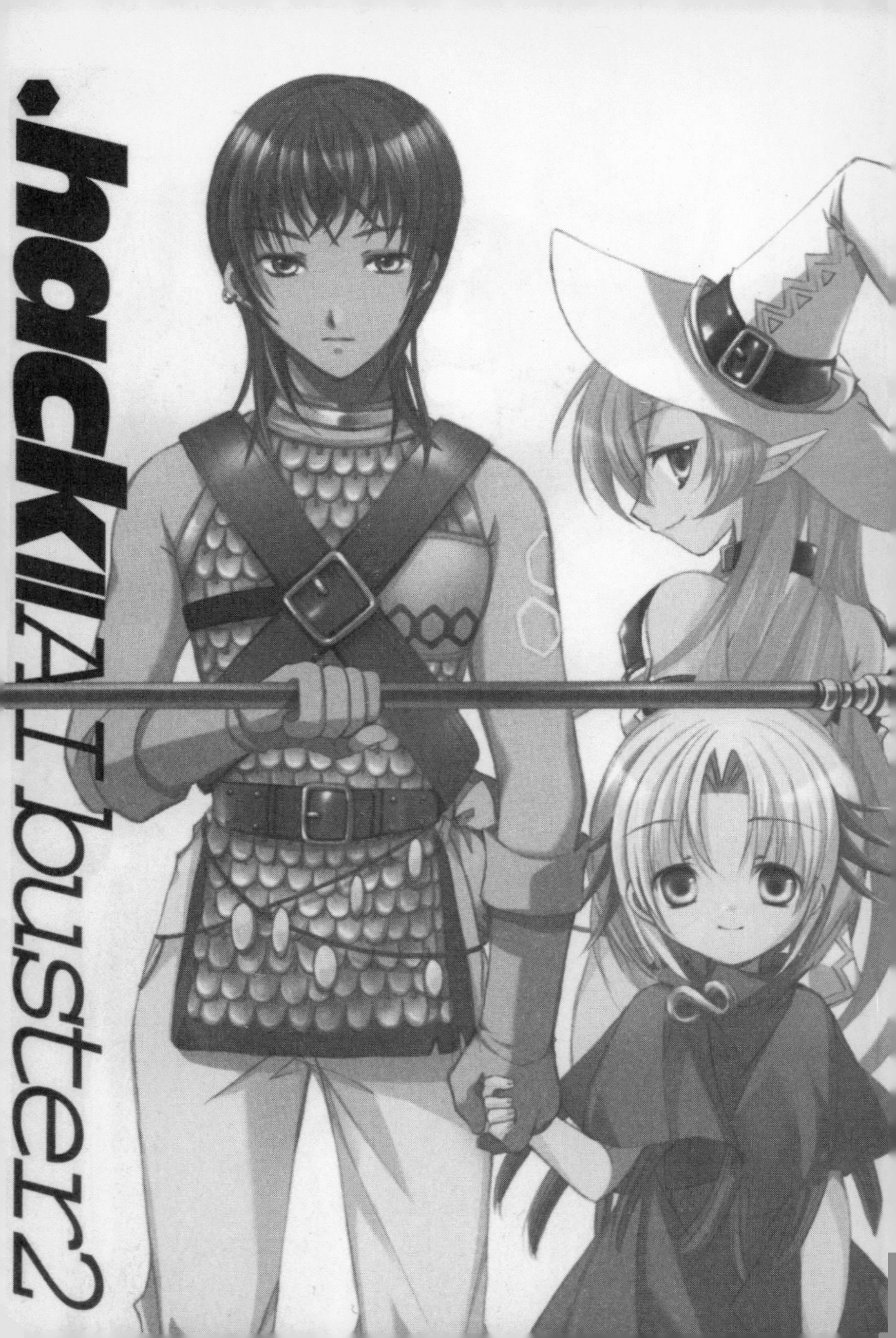
.hack//AI buster2

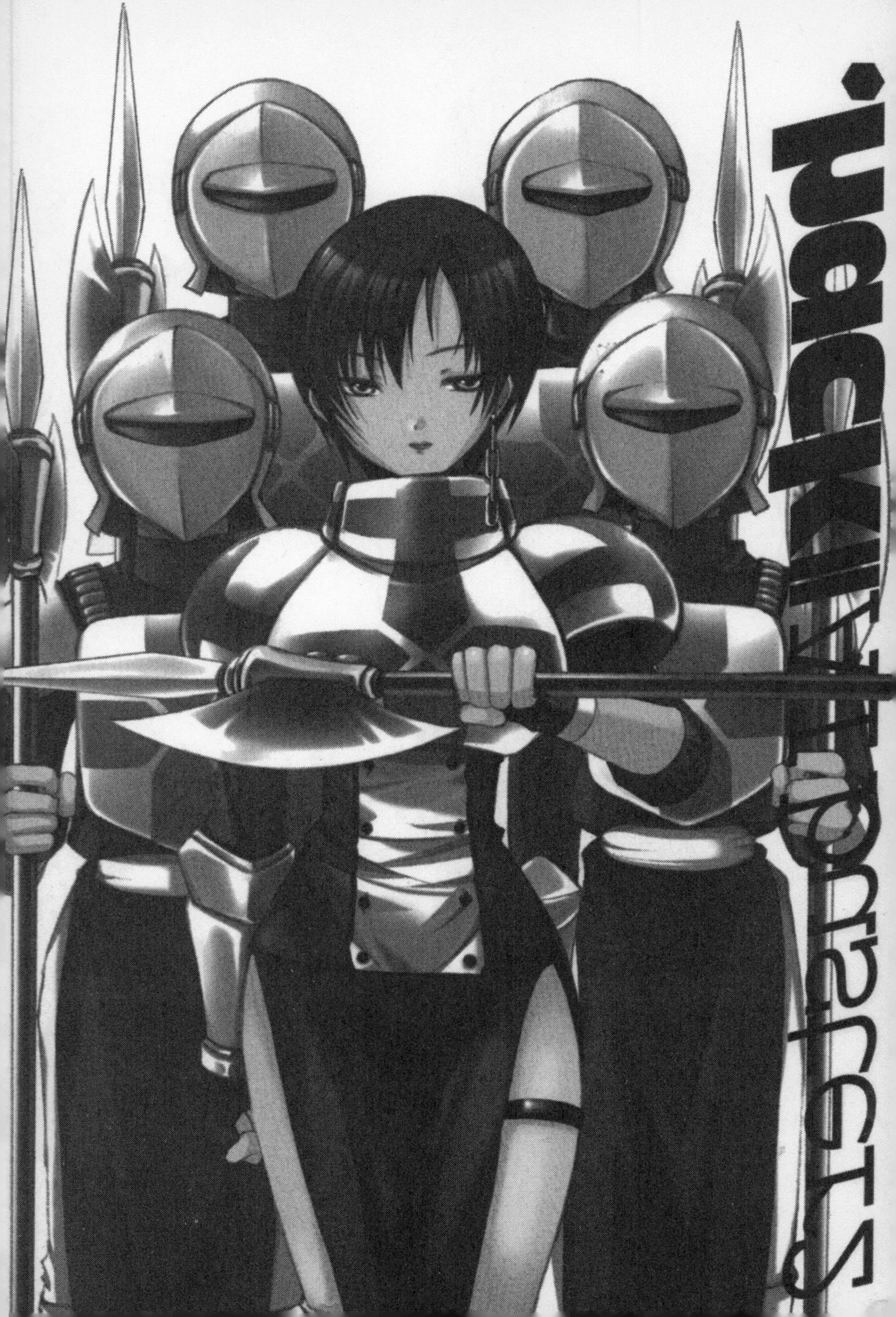

.hack//Ai buster 2
Story by Tatsuya Hamazaki
Illustrated by Rei Idumi

Translation - Duane Johnson
English Adaptation - Stormcrow Hayes
Copy Editors - Eric Althoff and Hope Donovan
Design and Layout - Jose Macasocol, Jr.
Cover Design - Christian Lownds

Editor - Nicole Monastirsky
Junior Editor - Kara Stambach
Digital Imaging Manager - Chris Buford
Production Managers - Jennifer Miller and Mutsumi Miyazaki
Managing Editor - Lindsey Johnston
VP of Production - Ron Klamert
Publisher and E.I.C. - Mike Kiley
President and C.O.O. - John Parker
C.E.O. - Stuart Levy

A  Novel

TOKYOPOP Inc.
5900 Wilshire Blvd. Suite 2000
Los Angeles, CA 90036

E-mail: info@TOKYOPOP.com
Come visit us online at www.TOKYOPOP.com

ISBN: 1-59816-407-4

First TOKYOPOP printing: February 2006
10 9 8 7 6 5 4 3 2 1
Printed in Canada

History of [The World]

End of the 20th Century

The U.S. Department of Defense develops the ARPANET, which becomes the basis of the Internet. By 1999, almost everyone across the world has access.

Beginning of the 21st Century

As the Internet increases in popularity, classified government information becomes harder to conceal and easier to obtain. Hackers continue to attack networks; cyber crime increases.

2002.10

The United Nations subsystem, WNC, is implemented.

2003.1

WNC winter meeting.

2003.4

A new virus called *Hello, WNC* infects up to ten million users.

2003.12

The Japanese youth who created the *Deadly Flash* virus is sentenced to death.

2004.4

At the WNC spring meeting, the following bills are passed: *Investigation and Research of New Viruses, Technical Security Development Aid,* and *Strengthening Reinforced Penal Regulations of Net Crime.*

2004.8

Emma Weilant dies.

The net poem *Epitaph of Twilight* is lost before it can be completed.

The Swiss Bank's main computer gets hacked, losing more than $84 million.

2005.1

Hacking causes the New York Stock market's prices to hike.

2005.12

On December 24th, *Pluto Kiss* shuts down the Internet; all network computers and communication control systems crash, only to recover 77 minutes later. A 10-year-old elementary school student causes the virus.

2006.1

America's 44th president, Jim Stonecold, resigns.

ALTIMIT OS becomes The World's most commonly used operating system.

2006 Summer

CyberConnect Corporation (CC Corp.) takes over and becomes the foundation for The World.

Harold Hoerwick sells Fragment to CC Corp.

2007.1

The ALTIMIT OS Corporation (head office in San Francisco) establishes 12 overseas affiliation firms.

2007.5

Watarai and Junichiro Tokuoka begin work on the Japanese version of Fragment, which later becomes The World.

ALTIMIT OS' Fragment begins its test play.

2007.7

Fragment becomes the most popular topic among network game users.

2007.10

WNC announces that all computers switch to ALTIMIT OS.

On December 24th, the United Nations names *The Mother Mary's Kiss* an international holiday.

CC Corp. announces the release of Fragment.

2007.11
Beginning of the month

Within the beginning of the first hour, The World receives more than 100,000 orders.

2007.11
End of the month

CC Corp. denies the rumors of discontinuing The World.

2007.12.24

The World's Network Security Declaration President, Alex Coleman, is informed of the start of The World's download sale.

2010

While debugging, Watarai meets with the Vagrant AI. (Story #1, 2nd Character)

Watarai investigates the cat PC. (Story #2, Wotan's Spear, based on *.hack// Sign*)

The second Internet crash, *Pluto Again,* occurs. (Based on the PS2 game)

2011

Watarai leaves CC Corp.

2013

Saki Shibayama takes over as official debugger. (Story #3, Kamui)

Rena Kunisaki purchases The World. (Story #4, Rumor)

2014

.hackers Official Limited Edition Character Exhibition. (Story #5, Firefly, based on *.hack// Legend of the Twilight*)

Foreword

Welcome to The World!

Part of what makes *.hack* unique is that its universe is a combination of genres: fantasy/sword & sorcery meets cyberpunk meets RPG, with a little techno-evolution added to the mix.

Ever since William Gibson coined the term "cyberspace" in his 1980s novel *Neuromancer,* he created a new sub-genre of science fiction. Though arguably an inevitable genre given the rapid rise of computers and technology, Gibson was the first to give it voice in his brilliant novel, which mostly takes place in the Far East.

So, in many ways, *.hack* comes full circle as a story set in a game world from the Far East, finds its way west.

Each of five short stories in this collection is told from a different character's point of view, yet each of them gives us some new insight into The World they all share.

Though The World may be an online fantasy game, the adventures told within are more than mere hack and slash as the players encounter a growing number of AIs. It is up to the Cobalt Knights to find and delete all such anomalies, but what happens when the debuggers begin to question the validity of their mission? After all, are the knights merely debugging a computer program or are they executing a newly evolving life form? Can consciousness rise out of cyberspace? Watarai, the head of the Cobalt Knights, and his successor face these questions in the stories "Wotan's Spear" and "Kamui."

The first story "2nd Character" gives us a different perspective on volume 1 of *.hack //AI buster* as we now see the story through Hokuto's eyes. We get to learn about the woman behind the avatar and her personality is far from what you would expect.

Foreword

The final story presents a fairly clever riddle for anyone who has ever played any online game. The clues are all there, so can you figure out the answer before Hotaru does?

No doubt these stories will entertain, but they will also shed new insight into the *.hack* universe for anyone who has read the graphic novels, played the games, or has watched the anime. We hope you dig this book as much as we have. See you soon in *.hack//Another Birth!*

2nd Character/
Haruka Muzuhara's Situation

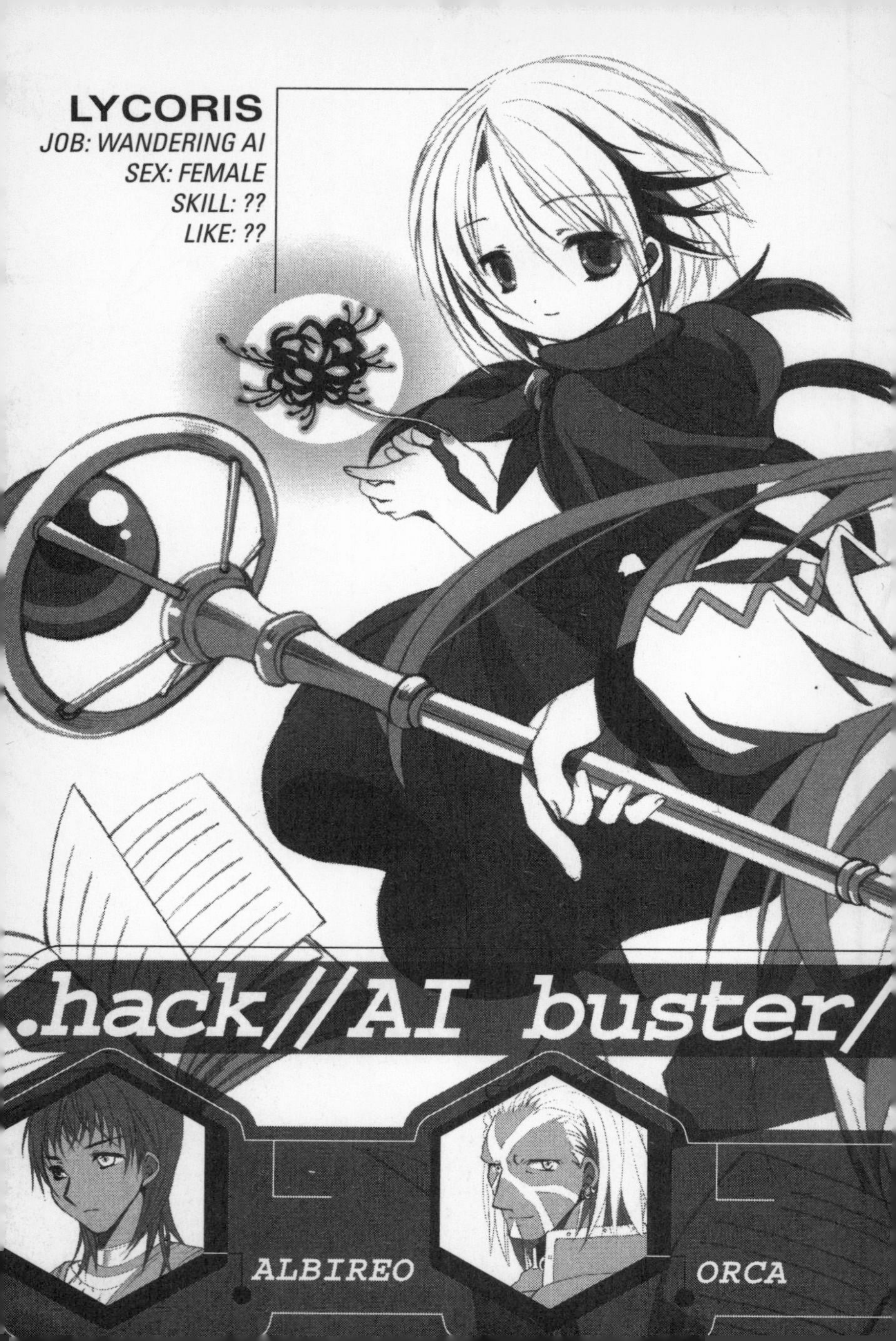
LYCORIS
JOB: WANDERING AI
SEX: FEMALE
SKILL: ??
LIKE: ??
.hack//AI buster/
ALBIREO
ORCA

HOKUTO

JOB:
WAVEMASTER
SEX: FEMALE
SKILL: BEGINNER
LIKE: POEM

2nd Character

BALMUNG

NO DATA

.: 1 :.

My place stank to high heaven. Why? Well, because I slept next to the garbage dumpster again. How could I be so lazy? More important, why was I such a screwup?

I walked into my workroom and stared at my two laptops. The faint glow from the screens cast eerie shadows on the wall. On one computer was a shareware text editor program; on the other, the *Reader's Plus* dictionary, with over forty-six thousand entries. Sitting on the corner of my desk were piles of unread Western books and other reference materials including *The Random House English-Japanese Dictionary* and *Sanseido's New Concise Japanese-English Dictionary*. I don't know why I kept the two dictionaries since I stopped using them long ago. The e-dictionaries, with advanced search functions and portability, were much more convenient.

I needed these books and programs for my job as a translator. Unfortunately, I just bungled my latest project all to hell, and my deadline was rapidly approaching. All I could do was stare at the clock, watching the hours tick away.

I sat down at my desk. In the spirit of procrastination, I clicked on the ALTIMIT OS icon and placed the goggle Face Mount Display, or FMD, over my head. The internal speakers vibrated with sound. For a moment, I was able to escape from looming deadlines and pestering editors and even my dark, cramped two-bedroom apartment. I was able to escape from reality and enter The World.

Mac • Anu

My avatar, Hokuto, was a cute, scantily clad teen witch with a pointy hat. She was known as a Wavemaster or spell caster. She was my second character and a novice. Because she looked considerably younger than me, I used special voice modulator software to make myself sound younger. Using these types of devices was part of the fun of role-playing in The World.

I had just logged in when I noticed a Long Arm (game talk for a spear user) named Albireo in the water capital of Mac • Anu. He stood on the second floor balcony of an old building situated along the river. It wasn't his character that drew my attention, but rather his spear. It was unlike anything I'd ever seen before, and I knew most of the weapons of The World pretty well. I zoomed in and studied its unfamiliar features and intricate markings.

I just had to learn more, so I pulled back far enough to examine the character who held the spear; he had brown skin and shiny black hair, trimmed in a wolf-cut. He wore a sleeveless scale-mail tunic, which meant he could've been a fallen knight. I didn't think he was a mercenary or a bandit because of his spear, which usually symbolized order.

My curiosity got the better of me. I had to know more about this weapon and its owner. I approached his home cautiously. The fact that he even *had* a home meant he was a wealthy high-level player. I was trying to think about what to say to him when the lively theme music for Mac • Anu abruptly stopped and switched to a dangerous battle song.

"Ah!" I uttered in surprise. The chat software picked up my voice automatically and displayed it as window text.

Hokuto: Ah!

How could I forget that today was the day of the Monster Invasion? Stupid, stupid, stupid!

Monsters usually don't appear in root towns like this one, but once a month, a massive horde of hideous creatures breaks through the spiritual barriers and attacks. Unfortunately, Hokuto, my character, was a first-level weakling.

Suddenly, several goblins appeared, each one glaring at me. I targeted the front door and quickly knocked.

```
Albireo: Who's there?
```

A familiar voice from the other side answered.

"Help!" I shrieked, panicking. "I'm being attacked by a goblin creature! It's about to kill me! HELP!!!"

A moment later, I met Albireo.

.: 2 :.

I felt like throwing up. I didn't want to return to reality and face all the work I had mistranslated. Anxiety gnawed at me.

I was plugging away on my fourth foreign novel, a book about terrorists in Northern Ireland. It wasn't a *horrible* mistranslation, really, but since I wasn't a terrorist and never had any aspirations of becoming one, I wasn't as talented as the IRA and SAS guys were with weapons and explosives. In other words, I didn't know what the hell I was talking about, or how to translate what I'd read into Japanese. Just because someone can *read* English, doesn't mean they can translate it well.

I felt depressed, or maybe I was just plain neurotic. But something was making me sick. I was nauseated, even though I hadn't eaten in days. Maybe I should eat something.

Instead, I went online.

I read through the BBS strings about literature. I used to post anonymous comments before I became a professional translator. Now, I was the one being attacked as multi-lingual readers picked apart my mistranslations in excruciating detail, mercilessly mocking my efforts. Ah, karma.

Their verbal knives slashed at my delicate ego.

If a translated book was well received, the credit always went to the author. But if the book didn't sell, then it was always the translator's fault. Readers only recognize translators when they screw up.

2nd Character/Haruka Muzuhara's Situation

I needed comfort. Real, warm, relaxing comfort. I wish I had a cat. Instead, I had the cold electronic filter of cyberspace to ward off loneliness and anxiety; I took to it like a junkie, constantly needing my fix.

While I surfed, I noticed that the proof sheets for a short novel translation (due in two days) were strewn in haphazard stacks around my desk. Even in the electronic age, the best editors still proofread with a ballpoint pen and good old-fashioned paper.

I needed to finish this gig and move on to the next novel, which was roughly five hundred pages. My deadline was in two months. I hadn't started. Of course I hadn't started, I'm a procrastinator first and a translator second.

I flipped through the scattered pages. There wasn't a single red mark on any of the proofs. I couldn't begin. I was scared, terrified that I might make more mistakes, mistranslate again. My biggest fear has always been failure.

After a while, my eyes glazed over.

At least I could forget my emotional pain when I role-played. I sought comfort by opening the door of The World . . .

The Girl in Red

It took some convincing, but Albireo eventually let me in. He actually ended up saving me from the goblins. Not only that, but he went on to challenge and defeat the boss monster in the Invasion event, which proved to me just how strong his character was.

When he finished the fight—which was bloody by the way—I hurried back and waited for him outside his home. I practically forced him to form a party with me. Once he did, I noticed he was holding hands with a little girl.

He had a child?

The girl wore a red dress with an adorable red cape clasped about her delicate shoulders. Her eyes were perpetually closed. It took me awhile to figure out she was blind, which was why Albireo had to lead her by the hand everywhere they went. Her name was Lycoris and she didn't speak, although Albireo seemed to be able to communicate with her somehow.

Since she only appeared when we formed a party, I knew she wasn't a normal player.

Albireo ignored my questions about her and said she was part of an event he was tied to, and she would remain with him until the event had concluded.

No sooner had he explained that, then two more peculiar characters arrived: Orca and Balmung.

Orca was huge and barbaric-looking, no two ways about it. Balmung, who wore gleaming silver armor, appeared more sophisticated, and what some might even call classically handsome. Neither of them could see Lycoris as we sat down together in a circle.

Albireo told me not to mention Lycoris. Of course, I agreed, but I had to wonder . . . Why did he want to hide her if she was just an event character?

Balmung and Orca had noticed Albireo while fighting the boss monster, and they were impressed with his skills. They came to invite him to their party to fight The One Sin.

In The World, The One Sin was known as the most difficult event ever created, and it quickly gained a reputation as being impossible to crack. Balmung and Orca came to request Albireo's help, but Albireo turned them down on the spot.

In the small talk that followed, Balmung looked at Albireo and said, "We recognize most of the weapons in The World just by looking at them. But yours . . ."

"You mean this?" Albireo held up his halberd, which was essentially a double-sided axe set on a long spear, adorned with beautiful decorative designs.

"Where did you get it?" Orca asked. "Is it a reward from an event? What's the name of the spear?"

I felt quite lucky; this was why I had come here in the first place. I sat back on my elbows and listened quietly.

"I'm afraid I can't tell you."

"Why?" asked Orca.

Yeah, why? I thought.

"It's a secret," Albireo said softly.

"Secret?" Balmung sounded skeptical, and frankly, I couldn't blame him.

Albireo shrugged. "I won't tell you. Let's leave it at that."

"I hope it's not a cheat item." Balmung murmured snidely.

Orca jumped in, "Balmung! Enough!" He turned toward Albireo. "I'm sorry, Albireo, he didn't mean to insult—"

"No," Albireo interrupted, waving his had. "It's a legitimate concern. I understand why you would think that, since I wasn't straightforward with you." He sighed and nodded to himself. "It's the Divine Spear of Wotan."

Everyone took a moment to process the information.

"The next question is," Balmung continued, "where did you get it?"

"He doesn't have to tell us that," Orca said.

I wished Orca would shut up. I'd been hoping that siding with Balmung would push Albireo for more information.

"No, it's all right," Albireo said. "I don't want there to be any misunderstandings between us. I'll be direct, but I trust I have your confidence with this matter."

They both agreed. I kept still.

"This spear is from the era of Fragment."

"You mean the beta version?" Orca's voice volume turned up a notch. "Albireo, you were one of the original test players?"

"Yes," Albireo said simply.

The beta version of The World, called Fragment, had a small, select group of roughly a thousand original test players. If the spear was that old, then it was truly a rare and unique item.

"Awesome! That's totally awesome, isn't it, Balmung?" Orca continued excitedly, "Did you know Balmung was a test player, too?"

Albireo frowned. "You were a test player for the beta version?"

2nd Character/Haruka Muzuhara's Situation

I could tell Albireo was extremely surprised—in truth, so was I! Out of millions and millions of players, what were the odds of *three* original players meeting like this? I wished I could chime in and tell them that I'd also played Fragment, but I forced myself to stay in character, maintaining the façade of a fresh-faced newbie.

"We're challenging The One Sin tomorrow morning at 9:00 a.m."

With a silent, somber nod, Albireo declined their invitation. I couldn't for the life of me figure out why. Even though he'd excused himself, claiming that he preferred playing solo, this was a rare opportunity. But I suspected it had something to do with the little girl in red. I decided to stick around and see what else I could learn about the mysterious Albireo and his ancient spear.

As Orca was leaving, he switched to Whisper Mode and said, "Hey, Hokuto."

I switched as well so Albireo couldn't hear our conversation. It was one of the unique aspects of gaming in cyberspace; you could have a private conversation in the middle of a crowd. It was almost like telepathy or something.

"What kind of relationship do you have with Albireo? He said the only reason you were in his party was because you were 'special.' "

I blinked, shocked. "He said I was special?"

I had wondered what they had been saying to each other in Whisper Mode. Now I knew they were talking about *me*.

"If he said I'm special, I can't deny it," I said boldly, to mask my discomfort.

"Do you two know each other in real life?"

"Yes, we're old friends. We grew up together," I intentionally misled him.

Apparently, that was all he wanted to know, and so with casual goodbyes, the two warriors left. Once they were gone, Albireo said we could talk.

He chuckled. "I'm impressed. You were surprisingly quiet."

"Because I didn't understand a word you said," I lied. I had to keep up appearances, especially if I was going to convince Albireo to keep me around. His spear intrigued me, especially if it was from Fragment.

I recalled an anonymous web posting that mentioned that the system administrators used a spear as a debugging item. If this information was true, it must have come from someone on the inside.

I wondered about Albireo's occupation in the real world.

"It's about time I drop out," Albireo said, then yawned.

I nodded, disappointed, but there was no reason I could think of for him to stay. But a few seconds later he still hadn't left.

"I can't logout," he said.

I thought he was kidding. I joked that he should call the system administrator, but he took me seriously and replied, "It isn't proper to call the system administrator for a troubleshooting problem. Besides, it'll probably fix itself in a moment."

"Maybe it's the girl," I teased. "Maybe she doesn't want to let you go, Al."

"AI? Who's AI?"

"You. Your name's too long and complicated so I'm going to call you AI. And I think I'll call her Lyco."

Albireo seemed annoyed. It was hard to tell, really.

But before he left, I switched to first-person POV and, for the first time, noticed his eyes. They were two different colors: one blue and the other yellow. I found myself becoming more intrigued with each passing moment.

.: 3 :.

I ventured into the fiction section of the local bookstore, bought a book on Celtic mythology, and read it that same afternoon—thus the birth of my love affair with Celtic mythology. Later, I checked out whatever I could from the local library; the Legend of King Arthur had risen in rank as one of my favorite myths. I didn't just stop at Malory or Tennyson, I went all the way back to the *Book of the Red* and the *Book of the White*, checking out scanalations of the ancient gilded texts.

2nd Character/Haruka Muzuhara's Situation

I eventually realized that the original Celtic folk tales were first translated into English, and then into Japanese. It was soothing to let the translated words flow into me, like listening to new age music during meditation. That's when I became interested in the person who translated my favorite books, which ultimately inspired me to become a translator as well.

I fervently studied to enter the foreign language university as an English major. Because Japanese translations of Celtic books were scarce, I wanted to learn English, so I could enjoy other Celtic books that only existed in English.

During this same time, I discovered William Butler Yeats. He had helped rejuvenate Irish literature, won a Nobel Peace Prize, and was one of the best poets of the twentieth century. I decided to base my graduate dissertation on him.

Unfortunately, I graduated with only average grades. In those four years, I realized that I couldn't find a job translating Celtic mythology. Basically, I was just a bookworm who wasn't interested in research or extended study. I loved books and stories, but I couldn't find any jobs with publishers. So I decided to put my English degree to good use (hunger was a motivating factor) and went to work for a small company in an administrative office that dealt with English literature.

After three tedious years, which all seemed to blur together when I try to think about them, I quit. I then worked temp jobs while I attended a weekly translation school. I tried writing novels, thinking that would be a good creative outlet, but never had the tenacity to finish anything. Suddenly, I was thirty years old and lacked anything remotely resembling stable career. My life had become a major disappointment.

Murmuring, Night, Alchemy

Even though it was a weekend, I should have tried working on my translation. Instead, I went to Captive, Fallen, Angel, to rejoin Albireo.

2nd Character/Haruka Muzuhara's Situation

I arrived just in time to witness Orca and Balmung defeat the supposedly invincible boss monster of The One Sin. But that's not why I shirked my workload. I wasn't interested in them or The One Sin. I came to see Albireo.

Why was I so obsessed with him? Perhaps I wanted to find out if he was really a system administrator. If the rumors were true and his spear had the ability to debug, then that meant Albireo really worked for CC Corp., which would also explain why he'd want to play solo (since employees probably weren't allowed to form parties with regular players).

But why was he playing the game at all? Was it a break from work? Was he debugging a new event? It was hard to determine anything about him at this early stage.

Then there was Lycoris.

Albireo was obsessed with playing through her event, which seemed less like the act of a system administrator, and more like a hardcore gamer.

Meanwhile, Lycoris was going through some bizarre changes as well. Initially she'd been blind, but now she could see. Clearly, Albireo was making progress solving her event.

And then something completely unheard of happened.

Normally, the only way to move through the different areas of The World was through a Chaos Gate, which were warp points with a three-word address that described the area to which you were trying to gate. But they were the *only* ways to travel between areas. Or at least, so I thought.

One moment we were observing Orca and Balmung in The One Sin, and the next moment, we transported to Murmuring, Night, Alchemy without ever being near a Chaos Gate.

Technically, it should have been impossible, but it happened. The only two ways such a thing could occur was if there was a glitch in the system or a cheat. And I didn't think it was a glitch. Unfortunately, since I was pretending to be a novice, I couldn't ask Albireo about this phenomenon. But I had to wonder if Lycoris was somehow behind it all, or if it was because Albireo was a system administrator and had special powers to move around The World at will?

Once we arrived, Albireo, Lycoris, and I played under the starry sky. It was a nice warm night, and we were all in a good mood. After a while, I could tell Albireo and Lycoris were speaking in Whisper Mode. Again, this was odd for a NPC, and I desperately wanted to know what they were talking about, but I couldn't hear a thing, and I knew it wouldn't do any good to ask.

I gazed up at the stars and thought about Albireo's colorful eyes.

.: 4 :.

Most people who read my translations before they met me were surprised to find out I was a woman. My name, Haruka, wasn't gender specific, and my translations tended to sound masculine, and, since most of the original authors I've translated were male, I was often mistaken for a man.

It was actually quite a compliment and, I think, one of the reasons I was selected as a test player for Fragment, the beta version.

It was this mistake that helped turn my life around. Shortly after I began playing, I joined a party that discussed foreign novels. We exchanged member addresses and became friends. When I told one of them that I had been attending translation school, she wanted to meet me in real life. When we met, I found out that she was the editor of a large publishing company. She gave me my first translation job.

I immediately quit my temp job and began freelancing. Unfortunately, it didn't pay well and it wasn't long afterward that the publishing industry hit a recession. But working from home was still better than waking up early and going into an office every day. Plus, it left me the freedom I craved to wander The World whenever I felt like it.

Of course, my boss played in The World as well, which caused difficulties when I was behind on a deadline. In fact, that's why I created Hokuto, so I could play in The World without being recognized by my editor. I've spent countless hours playing online since then.

But I still didn't give up on my big dream of someday translating a best seller. That's why I searched for stories in The World. I was looking for Emma Wielant. I made it my life's work.

Hidden, Forbidden, Sacred

The setting sun shone weakly over The World. The lake rippled with a gentle breeze. Clouds hovered on the edge of twilight . . .

"Where are we, Al?" I asked.

"It's the Hidden, Forbidden, Sacred Zone." His words felt as cold as the darkening sky.

We walked across a bridge and approached an old church made of gray stone and stained glass. The eerie silence was broken occasionally by the melody of pipe organs that bellowed deep within.

"This is a sacred place in The World."

"Why is it sacred?" I asked, curious.

"Because it's taken from the book. Have you heard of *Epitaph of the Twilight?*"

"Um . . . the what?" I feigned ignorance.

"It's an epic that was used as the basis for the background of the game world. It is the foundation of the story." Albireo's eyes swept the horizon.

Over the course of our many adventures, Albireo had recovered Lycoris' eyesight, and systematically set about unlocking the secrets of The World. Thirsty for more knowledge, I stuck close by him, continually asking him questions. "Who wrote it?"

"A German woman named Emma Wielant. She posted it on her website."

So Albireo knew as much as I did. I figured that if he was working for CC Corp., he might know more than me, but if he did, he didn't show it.

I tried to dig deeper. "So what happened to it?"

Albireo took a deep breath. "The original version is lost. The beta version of The World was released in May 2007. By the time the test on the beta version was completed in July, the rumors had already begun to spread that the game was based on the web novel."

"Emma's book."

"Right."

"You've been playing this game since it was a beta version," I said.

"Maybe I'm a cripple after all?" he joked.

I laughed.

"Emma's site had been shut down long before the rumor started," Albireo continued.

"Why was it shut down?"

"Emma Wielant had passed away by then."

So far, his explanation was everything you could get off the Internet. I needed more. "Go on," I urged.

"I gathered everything I could get my hands on about her or her book. From what I learned,

Emma disappeared from the online world around 2004 or 2005. At the very latest, she was gone by December 24th, 2005. Do you know the significance of that date?"

"That's when something destroyed the Internet, right?"

He nodded. "Right. The *Pluto Kiss* virus. For seventy-seven minutes, around the globe, all commercial activities that relied on the Internet ceased. It was a huge blow to the world's economy. Governments, financial institutions, transportation, businesses—everything stopped working. Data was corrupted and released, trains collided, airplanes crashed . . . it was apocalyptic.

"Even the Pentagon computers, which were thought to maintain perfect security, fell victim to the virus. Once they went offline, the military's automatic retaliation system began to countdown because the computers thought Washington had been destroyed. If the network hadn't restarted when it did, the world would have been destroyed in a nuclear holocaust. And do you know who the perpetrator of this evil virus turned out to be?"

"A ten-year-old kid."

"That's right. It just figures that he lived in Los Angeles. Nothing good ever comes from that city."

"Yup," I agreed.

"As you must know, most personal computers were also damaged. The amount of lost data is unfathomable. I was one of the victims."

"What happened?"

"I lost my nearly finished dissertation that I had spent months working on."

"Didn't you keep a backup?"

"I do now."

I laughed, but it was definitely not a laughing matter. The *Pluto Kiss* virus bankrupted the temporary staffing agency I had worked for. The entire thing was a disaster.

But if he was writing his college dissertation during *Pluto Kiss,* then he was probably in his late twenties, which would make him younger than me. I suddenly felt embarrassed role-playing a naïve teenager.

"Anyhow, prior to *Pluto Kiss*, people suffered viruses and worms all the time. Today that's unimaginable because of ALTIMIT OS."

"It sounds awful." I shrugged.

"That's why there aren't any copies of *Epitaph of the Twilight*. It was lost because of the virus, and probably Emma's disappearance."

"Weren't there any hard copies?" I asked.

Albireo sighed. "Apparently, Emma's site was set up to prevent people from saving, printing, or copying the pages. If there was a hard copy, she was the only one who ever saw it. The only other way would have been to transcribe every word of it by hand."

"That sounds tedious. No one would bother to do that. Especially when it was online all the time."

"Right. It was free to visit and read the site, so why bother?"

"So, it's lost?"

"Maybe not. Apparently, there was a passionate fan, someone who actually transcribed and translated the text into English. Whoever it was must've saved a hard copy because that's why we have Fragment, which we used in the beta tests."

"So who translated it?" Obviously, I had a professional as well as a personal interest in his answer to this question.

"Who knows. Someone online. Or maybe a group of people. Because we don't know, Fragment lacks authenticity. We're not sure if the English translation was based on the original work by Emma Wielant. And if it is, we don't even know how accurate the translation really is."

I'm one of the few rare people who collected the pieces of the *Epitaph*. My German was very basic, but I went through all the English, Japanese, and some German sites related to the story. I even had characters set up in foreign servers to collect data there.

"You mean it could be wrong?" I asked, probing.

"Translation is a very imprecise process." He definitely had my attention. "Inevitably, changes must be made to accommodate the audience and culture that the text is being translated for. Accuracy isn't always as important as relevancy and, in this case, storytelling."

He had such sensitivity regarding the subject. Could Albireo be a translator as well? He definitely sounded like he was in the business.

"But just because it's subjective," he continued, "doesn't mean that it's a mistake. For example, a joke in English might not translate because of the difference in culture or language. Some words sound the same, yet they have two different meanings. But just because two words sound the same in one language, doesn't mean they will in another.

"Humor often plays with these subtleties that simply can't be captured in direct translation. So instead, the translator will try to keep the context of the scene, but change the way it's written to keep it interesting for the new readers. Otherwise, if it was kept exactly the same, it might not even be readable."

"You're right," I said, trying not to let on that I was starting to have feelings for him. For some reason, it was becoming more and more difficult for me to continue role-playing my second character, Hokuto. I was starting to act more and more like my first character, Haruka.

"But if the translator goes too far, then the original intention gets wiped out. That's not good for either the reader or the original writer. Words are very delicate. Keep that in mind."

If only he knew how much I agreed with him. But I needed to learn what else he might know. "But you said The World is based on the *Epitaph*."

"Yes."

"So how did they read it?" I asked.

"CC Corp. apparently receives thousands of emails each day asking that same question."

"And their answer is?"

"They never respond."

"Why not?"

"Well, we have to go back for a moment. The English version of the *Epitaph* begins with a scene at the 'Navel of Lake.' That's where we are now.

"Navel?" I asked, even though I knew exactly what he was talking about. I'd even visited the church in previous versions.

"It means center. I know it's odd phrasing, but that's how it was translated. Can't be helped. Anyway, the original story was so powerful, that even a snippet still drew people in. I know it worked on me. I was totally immersed in The World and wanted to visit it if it was at all possible. That's what inspired this place. Well, not just this place, but the entire game.

"I know when I was younger, I would take the different story fragments and try to piece them together into a more coherent arc. I even tried to learn more about Emma Wielant, so I might understand The World better than anyone else."

I felt as if he and I might be soul mates, we thought so much alike. I was hanging on his every word. "I wonder if I'd enjoy reading the *Epitaph*."

"I don't know."

"I thought you said it was fascinating."

"It is. But it's also very heavy."

"You mean it's thick?" I asked, for some reason still enjoying teasing him with my false ignorance.

"Not exactly. Well, it is, but that's not what I meant. The content is very heavy. It's not for everyone. I'm not sure it would sell very well if it was released. Even J. R. R. Tolkien's *Lord of the Rings* trilogy was only read by a small number of devoted fans in Japan before they turned it into a movie."

I loved Tolkien, but I didn't want to let on how much of a nerd I was. "But hasn't the *Epitaph* become just as famous because of the game?"

"Sure. But you don't need to be a fan of the story to be a fan of the game. The two are different. And yet, they're the same. I can't help but think that Emma would be gratified to know that her story lives on and changes daily."

"That is a rather sweet thought."

He nodded solemnly. "She's been immortalized, even if most of the players have never heard of her. The images from her imagination will live on."

I followed Albireo into the church. We walked toward the large window, under the four swinging pendulums, and down into the main hall.

We stopped in front of the altar.

"Please, Albireo," Lycoris said, suddenly standing behind Albireo.

"Hey, Lyco spoke," I said, surprised. That was the first time I had ever heard Lycoris say anything.

"You haven't noticed?" Albireo asked softly.

"Noticed what?"

"Voice chat automatically gets switched in any church from Party Mode to Talk Mode."

My eyebrows shot up. "Why does it do that?"

"It's not permitted to hide anything before God." Albireo turned and faced Lycoris. "I brought you here for a reason."

"Al, what's going on?" I was confused. I didn't know what he was talking about.

"Do you really want the item I obtained from the spring demon?" he asked.

What item? I had no idea what he was talking about. His avatar wasn't holding anything, but I couldn't look at his item list.

A beam of light from the upper story window fell squarely on Lycoris' face. She appeared almost angelic, otherwordly, ethereal, even, as she looked up in wide-eyed innocence and begged:

```
Lycoris: Please, Albireo. Please give me
         the yromem.cyl.
```

My part of the adventure ended there. A moment later, Albireo and Lycoris disappeared in a blaze of light, once again breaking the rules of The World.

Their sudden disappearance left me yearning for some sort of closure. I decided to write Albireo an e-mail. If possible, I wanted to meet him in real life.

Albireo,

You and your words touched my heart. You have become special to me and I'd like to meet you. I hope, perhaps, that you feel the same way. I don't know where you and Lyco disappeared to, but I don't want to end our adventure like this. Please contact me.

My mouse hovered over the "send" icon, but instead, I clicked "delete." I was hoping for too much.

I logged off as Hokuto and returned to the character selection menu. Moving my cursor past Hokuto, I chose the character below.

Instead of writing an e-mail, I composed a poem using words only he and I would know. Because, like me, he was obsessed with the game, I knew he would find the posting.

I signed it using the name of my other character.

Subject: The One Sin

Message by: W. B. Yates

Damage done to the evil shaped one,

too massive to compare.

Balmung of Azure Sky,

Orca of the Azure Sea,

together they gallop at full speed.

In the depth of my bosom,

your names shall remain.

You are none other than

the descendants of Fianna.

Together with the warrior

who wears the eyes of the stars.

W. B. Yates

After I sent my poem to the BBS, I logged out.

I was tired. The torture of facing my mistranslations and the guilt of an upcoming deadline loomed, but for some reason I felt satisfied. The work could wait. It would have to; I was exhausted.

I pulled out a gift from my editor: Irish poteen. It was ninety proof and until ten years ago, illegal.

I took a giant swig and crawled into bed.

As I awaited Albireo's reply, I started to drift off. I felt happy. Even though I knew my editor waited impatiently for my translations, I didn't care.

Wotan's Spear

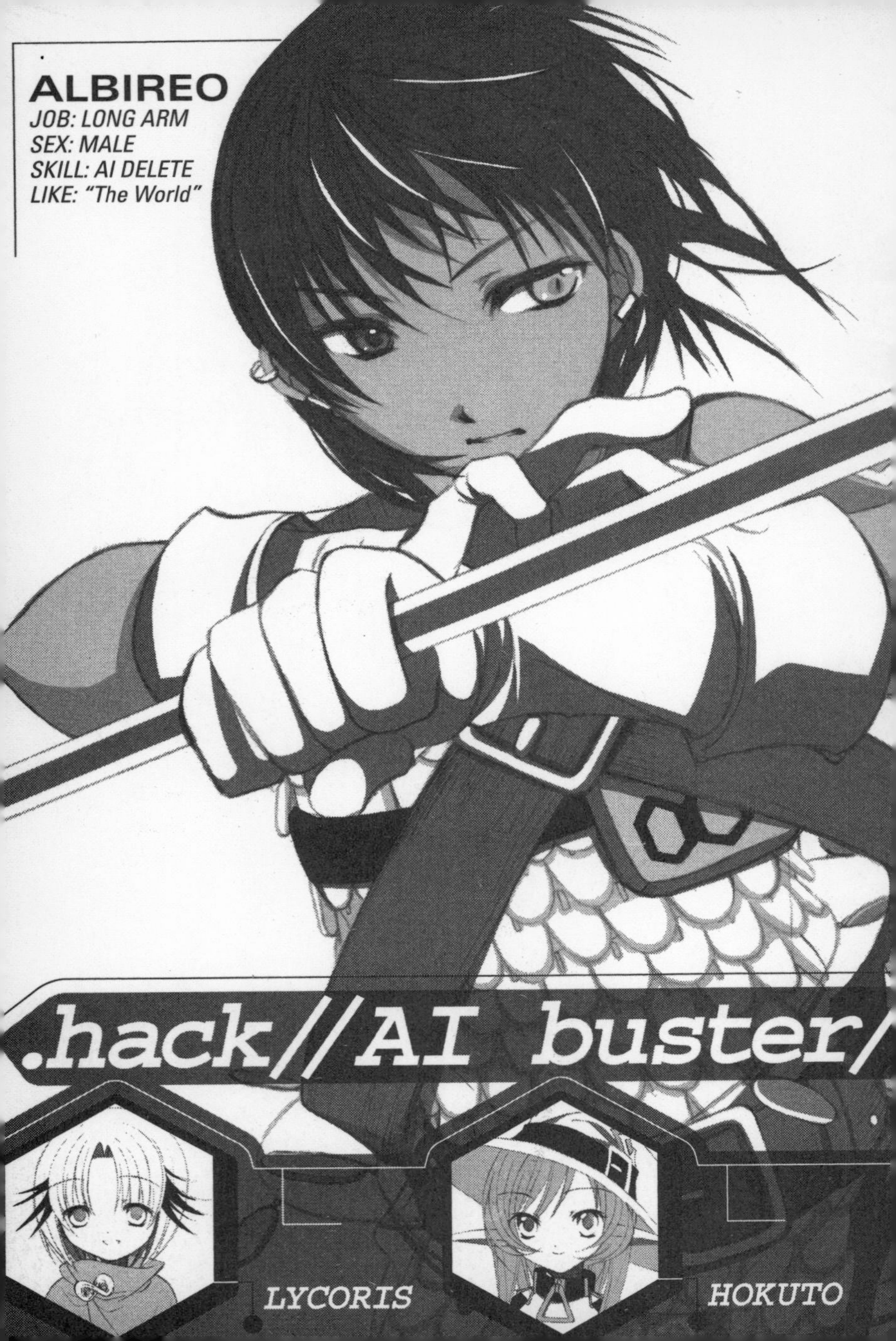
ALBIREO
JOB: LONG ARM
SEX: MALE
SKILL: AI DELETE
LIKE: "The World"
.hack//AI buster/
LYCORIS
HOKUTO

MAHA
JOB: WANDERING AI
SEX: ??
SKILL: ??
LIKE: ??

Wotan's Spear

TSUKASA   NO DATA

The red spider lilies
Are the color of fire.
Dare not touch them
The consequences are dire.

.: 1 :.

I love cats, but when a cat shows up in The World as a possible cheat or Vagrant AI, all my warm fuzzy feelings go out the window. Reading through the report that Saki Shibayama just handed me, I had a feeling that's exactly what I was dealing with.

I took a sip of warm coffee and tossed the report down on my desk. Saki nervously waited for my orders.

"Was there any user damage?" I asked.

"After a player traded with the cat, the player's data was destroyed. We already have several other similar complaints." Saki shifted her weight uncomfortably.

I leaned back in my chair and stared out the window. On the streets below, a mass of people rushed home from work. After reading the report, I knew I wouldn't be leaving the office any time soon.

Working in the Japanese corporate office for Cyber Connect Corporation (CC Corp.) had its advantages and disadvantages. Long hours maintaining the world's largest online game with over twenty million users was often a hassle.

"Does it speak?" I asked.

"What?"

"Does the cat speak?" I tapped my fingers on the report.

"I don't know. At this point, we're not sure if the cat is a PC or an NPC."

Saki was nervous because I had scolded her a month earlier for not memorizing the System Administrator User Manual. Every member of the Cobalt Knights, or debuggers, needed to know every chapter and verse of that book. As punishment, I had her making copies and fetching coffee and any other grunt work I could drum up. Now that she'd returned to her normal duties, she was still skittish around me.

I tapped my chin. "If the problem is a player character, then the game masters would eliminate him or her from the system. If this cat is a Non-Player Character, then it's our problem. Since we don't yet know what we're dealing with, we need to look into this further. Maintain contact with the GMs."

"Yes, sir," she said.

I hoped this rookie wouldn't screw up again.

.: 2 :.

I couldn't get Lycoris out of my mind. She called herself a failure, lost her will to continue, and chose to become a wallflower in The World. She left a deep impression on my heart, but I couldn't afford to be distracted by her now. It was time to go to work, and I had a new problem that needed my utmost concentration.

I logged in.

The best way to quickly learn what's going on in The World is to stand on the bridge that arches over the canal in Mac • Anu. From there, you can overhear the other players talking as they pass. As soon as I arrived, I managed to eavesdrop on this conversation:

"Did you hear that the Captain of the Crimson Knights got knocked out?"

"Did a Player Killer get him?"

"No, it wasn't a PK, he was knocked out in *real* life."

"In real life? What are you talking about?"

"He had it coming," someone else chimed in. "The way they go on about morals and justice is so annoying! I wish all of them would get erased from The World."

"You shouldn't complain so loud. Their headquarters is here in Mac • Anu."

"Whatever. They aren't the system administrators, so there's nothing to be afraid of."

The Crimson Knights, a self-governed organization of volunteers who mediated troubles and investigated illegal activities in The World, saved the system administrators from having to barge in all the time for the smallest indiscretion. After all, some incidents could be resolved between the players themselves. In fact, some players hated the Crimson Knights for taking it upon themselves to act as mediators, but they were officially recognized by the CC Corp. as a valid organization, which meant they had to be taken seriously.

They took their name from the book the *Epitaph of the Twilight*, on which The World was based. However, in the original text, the Cobalt and Crimson Knights were diametrically opposed, representing the forces of light and darkness. In The World, however, the two groups had little contact with each other and conducted very different missions.

"So what happened to him?" someone else asked.

"I don't know. He got into some kind of battle with a Wavemaster who controlled a monster, and the creature kicked his butt."

"What?!"

"But how did he get knocked out in real life?"

"I don't know, but as soon as his character was defeated, the player passed out at his terminal."

"That's ridiculous."

"It's true."

"That's impossible! How could you pass out in real life just because you lost a battle in the game?"

"I don't know. From shock, maybe."

"That's stupid."

"Look, all I know is, it happened.

"You can't believe every rumor you hear, Akira."

"If you don't believe me, look it up for yourself. It's posted all over the Internet."

Suddenly, I was confronted with yet another problem. I scanned through all the chats and BBS postings describing the incident, along with the actual e-mail being passed between the Crimson Knights. After twenty minutes of investigating and tossing out wild speculations, I was able to put together a rough composite of the events.

A Wavemaster named Tsukasa had a monster that, however ridiculous it may sound, was described as resembling a golden dumbbell. When the Captain tried to fight the monster, the creature clobbered him, and the person controlling the avatar—a reasonably healthy twenty-year-old—collapsed into a catatonic state, only to wake hours later with severe memory loss.

Past reports have described similar incidents—players passing out from exhaustion, or even occasionally dying from playing for too many hours. That's why CC Corp. followed strict regulations regarding the addictive nature of online games. Ultimately, though, every player was responsible for their own actions.

Nevertheless, this situation could cause a panic among players. I needed to deal with the predicament as quickly as possible. Suddenly, I had a new mission. The cat would have to wait.

The first thing that had me confused was the fact that the *player* controlled the *monster*, a monster that never existed before in The World. Though some spell commands allowed creatures to be summoned, they were very specific creatures, ones that we've seen often.

This led me to the second problem: the nature of the monster. Its description didn't match any characteristics of the monsters programmed into the game. It was something new, something totally unique, which could only mean one thing . . . whatever it was—PC, NPC, or Vagrant AI—it was an illegal program.

Now it seemed I had an illegal player controlling an illegal program. Great. But who was the controlling player, Tsukasa or the dumbbell monster? And who or what was the bug that manipulated the game this way?

Lycoris conversed like a human, even though she wasn't human. Appearances were deceiving. Determining real identities would be difficult.

I walked toward the Chaos Gate and noticed several Crimson Knights standing guard. They were looking for Tsukasa. The Crimson Knights didn't have the same resources as the Cobalt Knights. They could only set up guard posts along the gateways and hope that Tsukasa would walk on by. I had a different plan. Instead of waiting for Tsukasa to show up, *I* was going to find *him.*

.: 3 :.

My report on the Lycoris incident was sent to upper management, but I had omitted several details, including my final conversation with Lycoris and her secret hiding place.

The memory of her face as she spoke to me still haunted me.

"As long as I exist, Morgana will continue to whisper my location to you, until I'm deleted. But that's over now. I've given up."

"But why?" I asked.

"I am the product of a failed dream. I must die. I have failed to achieve his dream. Therefore, I'm afraid this is the end of your event with me."

But the encounter was too real, her death too meaningful. I wallowed in regret, thinking that there had to be a better conclusion, a different way to end the event. But just like in life, there was no reset button. I couldn't replay this moment in the hopes of finding a happier ending.

I was reacting as if she had died in real life. In fact, her passing affected me more than the death of my own grandmother a few years ago. Was I going crazy?

I had begun to question everything: What were the rules? What was the system? What was the meaning of my encounter with Lycoris? Where was God? Lycoris had tried to answer that last one for me.

"Morgana Mode Gone."

"What?"

"That's the name of God, Albireo. It's what lurks in the Inner World, which Harald attempted to create. God exists. God gave you the Divine Spear of Wotan and sent you the message telling you where I was. God tried to delete me."

"God . . . tried to delete you?"

She looked so sad. "That's right. I am an unwanted child. Even God doesn't want me."

"I don't understand."

"I was hiding from Morgana, not you."

The conversation ran through my head as I thought about The Divine Spear of Wotan. It was an item specifically designed for debugging, designed to delete Vagrant AIs. I'd obtained it during the beta version of The World. But who provided the spear? According to Lycoris, God created the spear in order to protect The World.

By God, did she mean Harald Hoerwick? He was the original programmer of the beta version of The World, the authority on AI research, and an all-around genius.

Originally, the game data of the The World was stored in the Harald system, a blackbox folder to which Harald attached a lock. Few knew of the folder's existence. Actually, only those who were deeply involved with the game's development had ever heard of it. When I found out about the system, I had to sign a confidentiality agreement.

Perhaps Vagrant AIs came out of the Harald system, which would mean Harald and Morgana were the father and mother of Lycoris. But then why would Morgana want to delete her own child? Did Harald intentionally include a contradictory idea in the program?

I just couldn't wrap my head around whatever technological alchemy he was trying to accomplish in The World. The only certainty I held on to was that the spear was created to protect The World and as a knight, I was sworn to that duty—even if it meant the death of Lycoris.

.: 4 :.

Colorful kites danced on the wind. Located on a steep mountaintop, Dun Loireag seemed to float above the clouds.

"Long time, no see," Hokuto said as she smiled with the command "/smile."

Hokuto was the only other character who had witnessed Lycoris. Other than an occasional e-mail, this was our first meeting since we separated at the Hidden, Forbidden, Sacred Zone.

"I was surprised you wanted to see me, Al."

"I requested to meet your main character."

"W. B. Yates felt that Hokuto should come."

I shrugged. "I guess it doesn't matter as long as it's you."

Hokuto was far calmer than in our previous encounter. Now that I knew her secret, that she was the web poet Yates, she stopped role-playing as a newbie.

"Do you have any information regarding the cat or a Wavemaster named Tsukasa?"

"You don't waste time, do you?" she laughed. "Don't I even get a 'hello, how are you?' "

I sighed. "Hello, how are you? Now if you're done playing games, tell me what you know."

"Have you seen the boards lately? Don't you know what everyone's asking about?"

"What?"

"They want to know how a character obtains a monster-handling skill. That's all anyone cares about— how can they do what's never been done. How they can get something new?"

"That's not surprising."

"But hardly anyone cares about what happened to the player who got knocked out. Now that's news!" She paused. "Well, I shouldn't say no one cares. Ever since the Captain was defeated, I hear criminal acts are running rampant."

Rampant? "What are your thoughts on this matter?"

"I talked to one of my contacts in the Crimson Knights, Lady Subaru. She knows the player behind the Captain in real life. Anyway, his injuries weren't as bad as everyone's saying. He's already back online trying to hunt Tsukasa down. Supposedly, the two of them talked to a player who said he could contact Tsukasa."

"Really?"

The Crimson Knights hadn't bothered to inform me of this new development. Perhaps they were taking it personally and wanted to handle it themselves. I could understand the sentiment, but I doubt they had any clue what they were really up against.

"What was the player's name?" I asked.

"I don't know. But a few days ago, one of the Crimson Knights spotted Tsukasa during their watch. Tsukasa slipped through the gate and contacted one of the players in the area a few days later."

"On the Dun Loireag server?" I asked, shocked. "How?"

What Tsukasa had done, jumping from one server to another, was impossible to do in the current system, which meant Tsukasa had somehow bypassed the system altogether.

"I don't know. But during their conversations with this player, an item was brought up. Have you ever heard of it?"

Hokuto typed in the name:

Hokuto: Key of the Twilight

"It's bogus," I muttered.

"So you do know of it! Well, you are a heavy player from the beta version, aren't you, Al?"

Hokuto didn't know that I was a system administrator. Or, at least, if she did, she never mentioned it. It was considered taboo to ask real-life questions online. No matter how close you became in cyberspace, the moment you asked to meet in real life, the relationship usually dissolved. I had additional restrictions placed on me, since there were corporate rules against debuggers ever meeting players, so I did my best to remain aloof.

She continued, "The Key of the Twilight is rumored to help bypass the system. I read the it on a German BBS. Do you want me to translate it?"

"You can translate?"

"I sure can. I'm so cool, aren't I?" I could almost sense Hokuto's player beaming with delight behind her FMD.

"I'm not interested in false rumors."

From a player's viewpoint, it made sense that Tsukasa had an illegal item that could bypass the system. But the Key of the Twilight was a myth. There were no items like that in the current version of the game.

"A system administrator!" Hokutu shouted, seemingly out of the blue.

"Huh?" My heart stopped for a moment.

"CC Corp. could send a system administrator to look for a logged-in user, right? And they'd have personal information from each player's registration. If Tsukasa was a cheat character, then they could restrict his access."

"True."

"But since the company hasn't done that, Tsukasa hasn't done anything illegal—yet. So isn't it logical to think that maybe Tsukasa found an item within the system? It doesn't matter if it's called the Key of the Twilight or something else."

I stroked my chin. "It's not easy to restrict access and delete accounts. There are legal issues. CC Corp. would need evidence of a user agreement violation. Maybe Tsukasa is a Player Killer and the Crimson Knights are making up allegations for revenge. The real question is: how did Tsukasa control a monster?"

"You're starting to sound like a system administrator."

I smiled, uncomfortably. This woman was curious, tenacious, and way too smart for her own good. "Yeah, right. Anyway, I have to go. Thanks for the conversation."

"You're going already? But you just got here. Let's hang out!"

"I can't. I'm busy."

This was true; I couldn't keep on talking regardless of how much I'd like to stay and get to know Hokuto better.

"You just use me for information and leave. That's not fair!" She stomped her foot.

The main reason I wanted to talk to Hokuto was because she knew Lycoris. Against my better judgment, I had told her how Lycoris had changed into a red spider lily. I wanted to tell someone who would understand the significance of that.

"Lycoris," I inadvertently muttered.

"Lyco?" Hokuto asked. "What about her?"

"It's interesting that she chose to become a spider lily. They're just such peculiar flowers—blooming in the autumn and pointing their leaves toward the winter sun. In spring, while the other flowers bloom, they die alone."

"When I was a child," Hokuto said, "I visited my family's grave in the country during autumn. On the edge of the rice paddies, the red spider lilies bloomed so thick it looked like a red carpet. Since they were so pretty, I picked them and made a large bouquet. But when I returned to the house, my grandmother told me to wash my hands immediately because they were poisonous."

"I didn't know that."

"They say that when you see someone that you'll never meet again, spider lilies carpet the path in red."

I wondered whom I was supposed to meet on this path.

"Are you tired?" Hokuto asked.

I looked at her. "Me?"

"Yeah, your voice—you sound tired."

I guess I was. Ever since I started working on the development team for the Japanese version, I pulled a lot of all-nighters and sometimes would only go home on the weekends.

"Maybe you should rest? Do you have to work tomorrow? I don't know what you do for a living, but if you can—you should take the day off."

"Thanks for your concern, but I'm okay." I couldn't say anything more without crossing the line.

I logged out.

.: 5 :.

System administrators logged in to the online management room, which was like a virtual office in cyberspace. From here, CC Corp. employees, subcontractors, GMs, techs, test players, and any other employees could log in and receive instructions, in some cases without even leaving their home. This login terminal was where I met Saki Shibayama.

"I've confirmed that Tsukasa is registered in a valid account," she reported in voice chat.

It might seem odd to speak to my colleague (who worked in the same building and on the same floor) through an online voice chat, but for system administrators, The World was their workplace.

She continued, "Tsukasa has been logged in for over ten continuous days. The character is still out and about."

"Even online game addicts turn off their computers when they sleep. It's possible that the password has been compromised, enabling hackers to crack the system and illegally use the character."

"But in that case, sir, wouldn't the registered user report that someone has taken control of their character? It's hard to imagine the regular player not noticing the illegal use of their character for such a long time."

Provided, of course, they were still alive, I thought.

If Tsukasa continued to cause problems, then GM and upper management would consider the source of the trouble to be Tsukasa's regular user and take action to resolve the problem in real life.

"What is happening in The World, sir?"

"What do you mean?"

"There's so much going on right now, what with the cat PC, the monster handler, and the dumbbell monster. What does it mean?"

"Our job is to figure that out." I took a breath, telling myself she was still just a newbie. "As system administrators, we can access The World in ways that a player cannot, but we don't have a complete understanding of it, like a God would. We're not omnipotent."

I seemed to reference God more and more often these days.

I cleared my throat. "A massive number of entries are logged every day and temporarily saved, only to eventually be deleted. We can review past logs only up to a certain time frame. It's impossible to read every log ever saved."

"So we need to collect information first in order to determine how to sift through the massive amount of logs."

"Now you're getting it," I said to her somewhat sarcastically.

"We need to narrow it down."

"That's why the job of debugging The World causes eye strain, headaches, backaches, and simply never ends."

"Mister Watarai, everyone says you work too much. You need to get out more often and enjoy your private life."

I frowned. "Let's stick to the subject. Our objective is to make contact with Tsukasa. The usual method of reading logs won't work, since he's continuously logged in."

"Which means he has to be somewhere in The World right now . . ."

"Exactly. So let's limit our surveillance to the present."

"Huh?"

"When you're looking for something, don't focus solely on the target; it's too narrow a scope. In other words, we won't look for Tsukasa, but we'll look at the whole World."

"I don't get it. What should we be looking for? There are thousands, sometimes millions of players logged in at the same time."

"If you use a little knowledge and analysis, the rest is statistics."

A pregnant pause. "I'm not following."

"Start by checking for any players who've died, especially those with an 'unusual' death."

"Unusual, how?" she asked.

"What does Tsukasa do with the dumbbell monster?"

"Defeats other PCs."

"Putting motive aside for the moment, let's assume that this is the primary objective. The defeated Crimson Knight player was a high-level character, but the area he was defeated in—"

"Was a low-level area!"

"Exactly! His character would never die in that kind of area, so that's an unusual death."

"I get it! I won't look for Tsukasa, but I'll look for the victims."

"Right! Follow the trail. Now get to it."

Little did I know the payoff would arrive sooner than expected.

.: 6 :.

Logged in as Albireo, I ran across the top of the castle walls. I had to hurry. The killer wouldn't stay in one place for long.

Looking up, I could see the large moon peak through holes in the clouds. But for some reason, the moon itself seemed blurry and distorted.

My eyes felt strained and my head ached. Looking at the 3-D screen was just painful. I couldn't focus. The doctor said it was exhaustion from eyestrain. It was an occupational hazard, I guess.

I shut my eyes for a moment and considered why a system administrator like myself had to log in as a character to debug something. In the world of programming, it didn't make sense. Did Harald include the debug function as part of his game design? Is that why he created the Divine Spear of Wotan? As long as I held the Divine Spear, I had to accept debugging as my primary duty.

But Vagrant AIs weren't really harming the system, were they? They weren't breaking any rules. Lycoris never harmed the system. It was the system that decided when to create and destroy *her*. System administrators merely held The World together, ensured that things ran smoothly, but The World ultimately abided by its own rules.

I didn't have time to ponder this further.

I switched to third-person POV. My avatar, Albireo, now wore silver plate mail, the official armor of the Cobalt Knights.

I leaned over the castle wall and scanned the area. I gasped at what I saw.

On a wall below me were four dead female Heavy Axe avatars. Judging from their outfits and equipment, they were high-level PKK, or Player Killer Killers, those who hunted Player Killers.

They had tried to hunt someone down, but instead they were slaughtered. Their killer still stood over them. It had to be Tsukasa.

The moonlight lit the living and the dead in a soft, silvery glow.

The wall was too high to jump. Instead, I switched back to first-person POV and zoomed in on the gray Wavemaster for a better look at him. That's when I saw it.

Hovering over him was a strange looking monster, playfully swirling, like a dog running around its master. It really did look like a dumbbell! It was three or four yards in length with two golden globes connected by a central bar.

I turned my attention to the fallen characters and grew concerned. They should have logged out by now. Were they unconscious in real life like the Captain of the Crimson Knights?

Tsukasa could gate-out at any moment. I didn't have much time. I tried finding a way to get to him, but none was apparent. Finally, I called out his name.

"Tsukasa!" I yelled.

I was struck so violently, my eyes reflexively shut. When I opened them, I could see Albireo slammed against the castle wall. But how?

I stood up and gasped. It was Tsukasa and the dumbbell monster. They had somehow struck me from this distance.

Turning, I saw the third character in this puzzle, a humanoid cat wearing funny clothes, its ears sticking out of his funky hat. It resembled something straight out of a children's book.

Bowing like a gentleman, the cat introduced itself.

"Maha," it said, twitching its whiskers.

Maha's movements seemed too real, too fluid, for the environment. My intuition told me it had to be a Vagrant AI.

"Did you give Tsukasa that dumbbell monster?" I demanded.

"No," Maha uttered. "Don't bother Tsukasa."

I couldn't see Tsukasa on the castle wall below, and Maha blocked my path.

My hands, gripping the controls, started to sweat. "I must stop him."

"Too dangerous," Maha warned.

Why would a Vagrant AI warn me, especially as I held the Divine Spear of Wotan?

"It's my job," I said.

"Yes! Albireo's job is to debug!" Maha replied.

A shiver went down my spine. Maha knew my identity. It seemed logical, then, that the cat might also know about Tsukasa and the dumbbell monster.

"Why is Tsukasa continuously logged in? Or was Tsukasa forced to stay online?" I asked Maha.

By now, CC Corp. had restricted Tsukasa's Internet access, yet he was still online. It just didn't add up; somehow he bypassed the system.

"How is Tsukasa still online even after the access restrictions? How is he concealing his location?" I yelled to Maha.

"Don't bother Tsukasa," Maha warned.

"Why are you protecting Tsukasa?" I responded in turn.

I targeted Maha with the tip of the Divine Spear of Wotan. The cat raised the hair on the back of its neck, like a real cat.

"Answer me, or I'll . . ."

Before I could finish speaking, every image in my FMD contorted before me. Maha raised its hand to summon something, which took shape above. It was a dumbbell monster!

But this one was different from the other; this creature resembled a semi-transparent amoeba with a liquid-metal consistency.

"What will you do if I don't leave?" Maha asked.

I could tell it wanted to delete Albireo. I was infuriated by the threat.

"You will be deleted!" I yelled, targeting the monster.

The creature wriggled and howled like a beast. Spikes pushed out from the gel and closed in on Albireo.

I quickly selected "/delete" from the debug command list and struck at the creature. My dark-skinned avatar didn't hesitate to thrust his spear into its gelatinous form, but instead of dying, a flash of light exploded, followed by a shower of twinkling metallic fragments that floated through the air like snowflakes.

My spear was *gone*. Using one of its spiky tendrils, the dumbbell monster had shattered the Divine Spear of Wotan!

I looked around, but now everything had faded out, including the scenery. The World whirled around me and faded to white. As I fell, I saw a red moon morphing into a flower, the spider lily.

.: 7 :.

I opened my eyes to see Saki Shibayama staring down at me. Was she crying?

"Mister Watarai! Do you know where you are?" Saki asked.

The high-pitch sound of sirens assaulted me from every direction. As I tried to turn my head around, I could barely make out what looked like flashing lights. I was in an ambulance; a paramedic checked my vitals.

"What happened?" I groaned.

"I found you passed out on your desk!"

I sighed heavily. "This is the third time I've been in an ambulance."

"Huh?" she asked.

I felt delirious.

"You work too hard, sir. You almost never leave the office and you're too possessive of your projects. We want to help you, but you never ask for help. If you break down, you'll be left with nothing," Saki managed to say between sobs.

I wanted to calm her, but I was strapped into the gurney.

I tried to remember what had happened, but my mental synapses were fried. I couldn't properly conjure up my memories.

I waved Saki closer to me. "Tsukasa."

"Huh?"

I whispered so the nurse couldn't hear, "Continue surveillance on Tsukasa. But don't make contact."

"What do you mean? Did you meet Tsukasa?"

"I'll give the details to upper management. They'll come up with a response plan."

My body felt heavy. I knew if I closed my eyes, I would sink into a deep slumber and possibly never emerge. Then I remembered—Albireo's Divine Spear of Wotan was shattered.

My heart felt broken. I didn't know what to believe anymore. Was a real player manipulating Tsukasa's avatar? If so, who? What was that dumbbell monster? What was the cat? Who was I trying to protect? I no longer knew.

.: 8 :.

Though it was spring, the air still held the final chill of winter. As I fixed my scarf, I passed a little girl in a red coat, holding hands with her mother. I kept on walking.

I found Haruka Mizuhara waiting in the coffee shop, holding a caramel macchiato in one hand and a foreign paperback in the other. She looked up from her book and called out my avatar's name.

"Albireo!"

I was finally meeting the woman behind Hokuto. She was a translator, slightly older than me. I realized she used software to make her voice sound younger online. That sort of thing was common in The World.

We talked about the past for a while before she said, "You were the Long Arm with eyes like stars. You balanced the CC Corp.'s perspective as a system administrator with the perspective of an adventurer in The World."

"But when I met Lycoris, the stars collided," I said, almost without thinking.

"Everything eventually falls out of balance. Even binary stars," Haruka said.

"Because I couldn't accept the conclusion of the Lycoris event, I was no longer able to properly role-play Albireo any more," I explained.

"Because the spear of your heart was broken."

"That's why Albireo died." I sipped the coffee. It tasted bitter.

"Death in The World is a passing of two souls."

I nodded. "I thought about the spider lilies coloring the path red. I think that's the path Harald walked. He wanted to meet Emma Weilant, a woman he knew he could never again meet. So he weaved Emma Weilant's poem, *Epitaph of the Twilight,* into an online game. That was how Harald reunited with Emma."

"Albireo's death also left a deep impression on Hokuto," Haruka softly spoke.

"Really?" I asked, moved.

"Would we be meeting now, if he hadn't?"

"Of course not. It was against company regs." I looked through the window at the blossoming trees and sighed. "I gave a whole decade of my youth to the online world. As a creator, a system administrator, and a player, I did everything I could. I don't regret it."

"Good. You shouldn't."

"I accept the consequences of my breakdown. After all, it led me here. It led me to you."

She smiled shyly. "I think you should know, I'm a mediocre translator, and rather poor. I can't even cook."

"Huh?"

"I can't take care of you." Haruka laughed.

I blushed slightly. "Thanks, but you don't need to worry. CC Corp. paid well and I never had time to spend my paychecks, so I've saved most of it. It's a pretty hefty amount."

"Does that mean you don't need me?" she smiled shyly.

"We all need someone," I replied. "And you were the first person to decipher the meaning behind the stars in my eyes."

◆ ⬣ ◆

After a long hospitalization, I quit the CC Corp., claiming health reasons, but in reality, upper management blamed me for triggering the Twilight Incident.

When Twilight occurred, the Cobalt Knights were powerless to prevent the birth of Aura, the ultimate AI.

Only one question still haunted me in the aftermath of my breakdown, and I had plenty of time to mull it over while I stared at the ceiling of my hospital room: Why did Wotan's Spear shatter? After all, it was a divine item, preordained from the beta version, designed to remove any threat to The World. I can only speculate, but I believe that I had done the unthinkable. I had pointed the spear at its very creator. I had tried to debug the one thing that couldn't be destroyed, Morgana, the God of The World.

Kamui

RIN
JOB: WANDERING AI
SEX: MALE?
SKILL: ??
LIKE: YUKINO

.hack//AI buster/

ALBIREO   LYCORIS

KAMUI
JOB: LONG ARM
SEX: FEMALE
SKILL: AI DELETE
LIKE: ORDER

Kamui

YUKINO   NO DATA

.: 1 :.

I started my day with my normal drug cocktail:
Xanax, an anti-anxiety medication; Lexapro, an anti-
depressant; and most important, my nicotine patch.
I couldn't smoke in the office and I spent too much
time online to go outside and get my regular nic fix,
so this kept me going until lunch hour, and then until
the end of the day.

Since one of the side effects of my medications
was thirst, I grabbed a bottle of water and headed
for my desk. I walked through the rows of cubicles
that comprised the security wing of CC Corp., until I

found my way through the maze to my own office and sat down. Sunlight streamed through the windows.

It still felt surreal, taking over the office of my old boss, Kazushi Watarai. But I didn't have time to mourn his departure. It was now my duty and responsibility to handle security.

I put on my FMD, enabled the debug mode, and logged into The World.

It was my battlefield.

.: 2 :.

I entered the world of my avatar, Kamui, a Long Arm and Captain of the Cobalt Knights. Our mission was to delete bugs.

I searched through the dark dungeons until I found several Cobalt Knights surrounding a little girl. Her facial features were European and she wore a gothic outfit, all black, of course.

She looked so innocent. She reminded me of the girl in red, a Vagrant AI, who had once escaped from my boss.

"Captain," called out Magi, a Wavemaster with glasses. "We've confirmed it's a Vagrant AI."

"Useless data," I spouted, glaring at her as if she were a cockroach running across the kitchen floor.

The other knights, all Long Arms with spears and plate mail, cornered the barefooted girl against the wall. She appeared afraid, which was odd considering Vagrant AI's can't feel. There was no player manipulating her avatar. She was just a program, without any sentient life at the controls. A Vagrant AI was little more than a cyber parasite.

"Your orders, Captain?" Magi called out.

"According to regulations, this Non-Player Character is recognized as an irregular NPC that is not in the specification of the Japanese version of The World," I recited.

With a sudden clang, the knights, in perfect unison, lowered their spears and stepped forward. They targeted the little girl with their spears, debugging items held only by system administrators.

"H-Help me," the little girl pleaded, fumbling her words innocently. It irritated me.

"You don't fool us, AI!" I barked. "Delete her!"

I enabled the debug command. The spears thrust forward, and pulled away, colored with transparent blood. We had completed our mission.

.: 3 :.

I entered the Hidden, Forbidden, Sacred Zone and moved toward the church on the isolated island. Dark clouds covered the sky.

Once I entered the church, I heard the pipe organs echoing. I moved along the hall where four pendulums swung, marking time. Finally, I reached the altar. Every time I returned here, I thought of my old boss.

I met Watarai through a fluke of fate. I had graduated near the top of my class and after interviewing with CC Corp., I expected to work in their creative division. I was shocked when they instead threw me into administration.

Initially, I was depressed and didn't care much about my work or my performance, but Watarai, my boss, turned me around. He taught me the importance of debugging and working in the system administration section. He taught me the importance of the Cobalt Knights and our mission to remove any bug, no matter how small.

"In an offline game," he once explained to me, "a player can cheat all he wants and there are no consequences. It's no big deal, because he's really only cheating himself out of the total gaming experience. However, when someone cheats in an online game, it affects other players. Not only is it unfair, but it also destroys game balance."

Watarai's eyes gleamed when he talked about it. "When someone cheats, part of The World shifts; and the more cheaters, the greater the shift, until The World eventually becomes unhinged—driving away both players and business. So it's important, from both a business and gaming standpoint, to keep everything fair. We must not allow anyone to cheat. No matter how small the bug is, we must delete it. Because the system must run smoothly."

Watarai always made sure everything ran smoothly. As Captain of the Cobalt Knights, he ran a Pole Arm named Albireo. However, an incident in the church changed him.

It was here that he first encountered the Vagrant AI, Lycoris. It should've been a simple debugging task, but something had happened that day, which altered Watarai forever . . . He had failed.

The Cobalt Knights had chased and cornered the AI into the church, but somehow she had managed to defy the basic laws of cyberspace—and escaped.

At the time, I was a rookie and didn't think much of the failed mission. Watarai, on the other hand, became obsessed. He never left his office and hardly slept for days, until he tracked down and finally destroyed the AI.

I'm not sure what happened during his hunt, but afterward, he started acting strange. Worse, he started to break down mentally as well as physically. I also noticed that he talked more and more about God.

"Only God could be omniscient enough to understand and even interact with everything in the system," he once told me.

"God?" I repeated.

"At least what I call 'God,'" he clarified. "Even though no individual can ever grasp the system as a whole, it's still programmed for anyone to look at any of its pieces. The entire World exists in binary code and is stored in Akashic records. The World that we witness is displayed on a screen. It's not reality. We're witnessing the illusion of reality, what the Hindus call *maya*. It's really just a shadow world. But the system itself is alive, and constantly operating every moment of every day. I call that system God."

He continuously referred to God whenever he tried to explain The World to me, but he never seemed to be able to fully express his thoughts. Ultimately, he gave up trying, though I always wondered if he wasn't hiding something that he just couldn't keep secret.

"Kamui."

I turned to see who was interrupting my thoughts. I found another Cobalt Knight approaching. It was Yukino Makimura, a young woman who had only been with the company for a year.

"What is it, Yukino?"

"I'd like to discuss a problem."

"Can this wait until tomorrow?"

"No," Yukino mumbled.

I arranged to meet her in the café downstairs after work.

.: 4 :.

"I'm sorry to take time out of your busy schedule." Yukino placed a cup of coffee on the table and sat down.

"So tell me your problem."

She and I were the only two women working in the division, so I assumed her difficulties might be related to sexual harassment or something along those lines.

"What can you tell me about Vagrant AIs?" Yukino asked.

I wasn't really expecting her reply. "Vagrant AIs?"

"Yes." Yukino stared into her coffee.

This wasn't something we should be discussing at the company café. Vagrant AIs were supposedly made by hackers to invade The World just for kicks. But as far as I knew, even the CC Corp. didn't know how all Vagrant AIs were created.

"Why do you ask?"

"Before I joined this company, I was playing in The World."

"Of course."

Despite her soft and seemingly meek demeanor, her file listed her as a hardcore gamer.

"When I was a college student, I met a Vagrant AI," Yukino continued.

"How do you know it was a Vagrant AI?"

"I wrote about it on an unofficial BBS, and a techie contacted me and told me the description fit perfectly with that of a Vagrant AI."

"Did you report it to the system administrators?"

"No." She hesitated, but then continued. "I'm not sure if you'll believe me or not, but I was playing with the Vagrant AI."

"Playing?"

"Well . . . we talked."

I looked out the window; an uncomfortable silence passed before I turned and faced Yukino. "Many Vagrant AIs have the ability to speak. In fact, they've improved their speech abilities at an alarming rate."

"This was different."

"How?"

"*I* taught it to speak."

"You were teaching it?" I was shocked.

"Yes," Yukino nodded. "He memorized my conversations."

I couldn't believe what I was hearing. "Okay, let's put aside the fact that you, as a user, ignored your obligation to report a Vagrant AI and had chats with an illegal NPC. At that time, you were only a player, so it can be excused.

However, I have to know if you harbor any special feelings toward Vagrant AIs because of your experience?"

"Special feelings?" she repeated.

"You know, are you fond of them?"

"I don't think so."

"You realize that any emotional traits they display are merely an illusion, a copying of expressions like a parrot repeating what it's heard. An AI is only a bug."

"But is the existence of Vagrant AIs really harmful to The World? Maybe it's—"

"It's dangerous," I stressed. "There have been cases where players lose all their data after coming in contact with a Vagrant AI. You're lucky that didn't happen to you."

Yukino bit her lip.

"Look, our mission as Cobalt Knights is to protect The World. Vagrant AIs are bugs, nothing more. Do you understand?"

"Yes." She didn't sound convinced.

"So what happened to this Vagrant AI you met in college?" I asked.

"Eventually, it disappeared." Yukino shrugged.

I wasn't sure about that, but I could tell that was all I would get out of her. "Very well."

I said good night and left the café, my thoughts all in a flurry. I needed to reassess whether Yukino could continue in our division or not. If any corrective actions needed to be taken, they had to be done as soon as possible.

.: 5 :.

I hate cats, so it seemed rather ironic to me that the cat incident was the precursor to the Twilight Incident.

After the situation with the girl in red, the Cobalt Knights looked for a rogue cat that we couldn't confirm as a PC or NPC. The cat was accompanied by a Wavemaster named Tsukasa, and an unknown, dumbbell-shaped monster. Since the monster wasn't part of the standard game, it had to be some kind of an illegal creation, possibly even a Vagrant AI. My boss and I were investigating their questionable activities when he lost consciousness. I found him passed out on the desk I now sit behind. He was still logged in.

I often wondered what happened to him that day? What did he see? What did he experience?

He never answered any of my questions. Whatever it was had clearly changed him.

Watarai remained hospitalized for a long time, his body broken from stress and over-exertion. The remaining Cobalt Knights were reconsolidated under Ryos, the main system administrator.

Then the Twilight occurred.

.: 6 :.

We were powerless against the changes the Twilight caused. Too many alterations had occurred for it to be covered up as a version update, and in the ensuing chaos, the company fell to turmoil.

One major change was that the Cobalt Knights were exposed to public users. Once the secret of their identities was out, they were disbanded and their duties were reintegrated into various other sections of the company.

Watarai never returned to CC Corp. Rumor had it that he was forced to resign and take responsibility for the Twilight Incident. As if he was the one who caused it. It wasn't his fault, but the company treated him like it was and cut him loose.

But by far, the worst loss was the destruction of the Divine Spear of Wotan. The ideals of The World were contained within the Divine Spear. Though spears were provided to all the debuggers, only Albireo personified the core essence and true spirit of the spear.

Kazushi Watarai put his whole life into his weapon, and now it was gone, vanished from The World. It left behind a gaping hole in the fabric of cyberspace, and at the very moment we needed Albireo the most, now he, too, was gone.

Fortunately, Watarai's stories and lessons taught me how to become a Cobalt Knight. He had prepared me to fight for the future.

"It's your turn to protect The World," Watarai said to me when he turned in his letter of resignation.

Then he disappeared and disconnected. He sold his house and unlisted his phone numbers. Clearly, he didn't want anyone to find him. Of course, I could find him if I really wanted. After all, it's hard to disappear in the electronic age. I'm sure I could easily track him down, but I wouldn't. If he wanted to disappear, it was best just to let him.

But his absence troubled me deeply.

Sometimes, I wonder what I could have done to help him. Where did he lose his way? Was it the girl in red? Did she change him? At least that's where the trouble seemed to start.

He made a mistake—lost the girl in red and then started chasing ghosts wherever he could find them. He became obsessed. Naturally, when the mysterious cat appeared, he *had* to find it. He could have assigned the case to me or any number of other subordinates, but he took each case personally.

I think he was haunted by his failure.

Was that it? Was that what caused him to push himself so hard that he collapsed in exhaustion at his desk? What was he chasing when he fainted? What did he see that haunted him so terribly, he could never tell me?

I suppose I'm not much better. I've taken the weight of The World onto my shoulders, just as he did. I work long hours and accept too much responsibility. Will I meet his same fate? Will I someday come to understand what made Watarai, the man I most respected, disappear?

It was painful when he wouldn't tell me anything. Now I'm on my own quest to discover what drove him to quit.

He held everything in his heart. Is that why it was so easily broken?

Or did he disappear in reality because he's living permanently in The World he so loved? Was this the future he foresaw?

After the Twilight, the CC Corp. reconstructed a replica of the Divine Spear of Wotan containing the same AI-hunting, debugging skills. Once it was perfected, management came to me and asked if I would reorganize the Cobalt Knights. I became their new Captain and followed in my mentor's footsteps.

I chose the name Kamui for my new avatar. It means "power of God." I wielded the new spear with the intent to fulfill Watari's mission. I even gave my character two different-colored eyes, the same as Watarai's avatar, Albireo. It would remind me of my purpose.

When he walked away from me, the day he turned in his resignation, I whispered a promise to him. Even though he couldn't hear me, I swore I would do everything in my power to keep my oath. I promised I would protect The World.

.: 7 :.

I had assigned Magi the task of finding a Vagrant AI. She confirmed its existence and gave me its location. It was exactly where she said it would be—in an enchanted forest. He was a half-naked teenage boy, with butterfly wings and amber-colored eyes that twinkled.

The wings were a giveaway, as they couldn't be created for a character. He was definitely a Vagrant AI.

The Butterfly Boy was playing with a girl, a Twin User. The avatar belonged to Yukino.

They were laughing and whispering when I stepped out from behind the tree.

"Miss Shibayama!" she said, gasping. "What are you doing here?"

"In The World, I'm known as Kamui." I pointed the Divine Spear of Wotan at the Butterfly Boy.

"Why are you here?" Yukino asked in a shaky voice. She was probably plugged into The World from her home computer.

"We tracked your avatar," I answered.

"But this is my private—!"

"When you joined the debugging team as a system administrator, you forfeited your privacy. I'm sure you read the employee regulations."

In order to prevent the abuse of system administrator privileges, it was against regulations for debuggers to have a second PC on a different account or log in for personal reasons. Yukino was violating her agreement.

Magi had discovered that Yukino had used company computers to log in to The World with her private ID several times.

"Is this the Vagrant AI you were talking about?" I glared at the Butterfly Boy.

Yukino didn't answer.

I glared at her. "You're not a child. If you think you'll be forgiven if you stay silent, you're wrong."

Yukino continued sulking like a little girl.

"I know you didn't find it during your college years, because you created your current avatar fairly recently. Did you find it during business hours?"

"He didn't do anything wrong!" Yukino exploded.

"It doesn't matter if it's harmful or not. It's not even human. *We* don't determine whether it's good or bad." I was irritated with Yukino. She hadn't listened to a thing I had said.

"Please! Let him go, Miss Shibayama!"

"My name's Kamui! Now stop wasting time. I came alone to see how you would react, but I can see this won't end well."

"Are you going to delete me?" Butterfly Boy asked.

He stepped in front of Yukino as if to protect her. He stared at me with his jewel-like eyes.

"What are you doing, Lin?" Yukino asked.

"Stop acting human, AI!" I yelled.

"Is this my fate?" Lin asked. His wings fluttered and I noticed tiny glittering confetti sprinkling through the air behind him.

I targeted the Butterfly Boy.

He looked at the spear, surprised. "The Divine Spear of Wotan? I thought it had disappeared."

I looked at him in disbelief. How did a Vagrant AI know about this spear?

"You're surprised, aren't you, Miss Shibayama? He knew about the Cobalt Knights and the debug item."

"Yukino, do you want to explain this?"

"When I first found him, he was a little caterpillar. I came here every day to see him. I logged in from the company computers when I was too busy with work to go home. I was worried, so I had to come see him. He was dependent on me. Whenever I stood under this tree, he crawled down from the top branches. He was only a small insect, but as I talked to him, he learned to speak."

Yukino pointed to the large tree. I looked up. Hanging from a tree branch was an empty brown cocoon.

"What is it?"

"A pupa. Lin recently went through a metamorphosis. He has grown at a surprising rate, not only in shape, but in his conversational skills. Sometimes he says complex things that even I can't understand."

"Yukino! Your job is not to observe Vagrant AIs!" I pointed the Divine Spear of Wotan toward Butter-fly Boy.

He looked skyward and began to recite: "The night of the old God hath passed. And gaining twilight and new order, the new world was reborn. But why do people depend on the nightly power of the old God through the spear?"

I was bewildered by Lin's statements. He sounded like a poet.

"What are you trying to say?"

"Why do you want to delete me?" Lin asked simply.

"Because you're a bug."

"I am Lin. You are Kamui. We are both residents of The World." Lin reached his hand out.

"I am also Saki Shibayama, a debugger and Cobalt Knight. From my perspective, you are nothing but an illegal program."

"From God's perspective, the existence of you and I are blessed by this World." As Lin spoke, he grabbed the tip of my spear with his bare hands. Suddenly, I couldn't move my arms.

"What do you mean, 'God?'" I asked the Vagrant AI.

"God is The World," Lin answered.

"The World itself?"

"Yes. You who borrowed the powers of the old God should know that."

"Old God? Are you talking about the Divine Spear of Wotan?"

"Yes. The one that should be deleted is this false spear."

"Enough!"

I made Kamui fall back out of his reach and established some distance. I reselected the debug command.

"Why do you want to delete me?" Lin asked calmly, without fear.

"To insult the Divine Spear of Wotan is to insult me and my mentor, who dedicated his life to the ideals of this artifact! I was given this spear to protect The World and that's just what I'm going to do!"

I was breathing heavily, trying to calm myself down.

"You won't listen to my story, will you?" Lin stared sadly.

I told myself he only *looked* sad, he didn't really feel sadness or anything else.

"You're good at confusing people, aren't you, AI?"

He was trying to confuse me just as Watarai had been confused by the little girl in red.

"Please don't, Miss Shibayama!" Yukino cried out.

I ignored her and announced, "According to regulations, this Non-Player Character is recognized as an irregular NPC, who is not part of the specification within the Japanese version of The World."

"Am I not one of the possibilities of The World? It is your false spear that is the abomination. Destroy the spear and you will find your salvation. Destroy me and you only kill a part of your own soul."

I gritted my teeth. "If my soul was corrupted by bugs, then I would gladly destroy it."

"And what of *my* soul?" Butterfly Boy looked forlorn, but I told myself it was only an act.

"You have no soul. You're nothing but a collection of ones and zeroes."

"You're nothing but a collection of atomic particles," he shot back. "Does that make you more special than me? Does that give you the right to end my existence?

Besides, who are *you* to determine who has and hasn't a soul? After all, you carry around a mockery of the old Gods."

"I'm just doing my job."

"That's just what the guards at the Nazi camps said when brought before the Nuremburg tribunals. But you're probably too young to remember that, and we all know history repeats itself." He shrugged.

"I know what you're doing, but it won't work."

"I'm only trying to point out that my life has as much value as yours."

"No, you're trying to plead for your life by making me out to be the bad guy. But I'm no Nazi and I can't exterminate something that isn't even alive."

"Exterminate. Isn't that exactly what you're doing— exterminating what you only think of as a bug? How many generations of genocide will it take before the violence comes to an end?"

"You can argue all you want, but it's not going to stop me from doing what's necessary. It's time to debug."

"Even in death, my life has value."

I pointed the tip of the spear toward him. His smiling unnerved me.

"Stop!" Yukino jumped between us.

"What is the meaning of this?" I demanded. "Clear out, Yukino."

He turned to her. "Thank you, Yukino. Your love for me also has value. And so will the sadness you feel when I am gone."

"Lin?!" Yukino called

"Go ahead, Kamui. Use your power and delete me," Lin commanded.

"That is the mission of the Cobalt Knights," I said, shaken.

I activated the command and pierced him with the spear. He released a high-pitched shriek as he violently convulsed, and then shattered into luminous pieces.

The enchanted woods fell silent, as if mourning his loss. Only Yukino's sobbing could be heard.

● ◆ ●

Yukino's violations and her concealment of a Vagrant AI were reported to the company. I was surprised she wasn't fired. Instead, she was transferred to a clerical department that had nothing to do with The World.

Yesterday, I went to the doctor and had them increase my prescription. My headaches are getting worse, but they won't stop me. Nothing will stop me from my mission. Today, I will continue my hunt for AIs.

My mission is my only proof that I am alive.

Rumor

BRIGIT
JOB: BLADE MASTER
SEX: FEMALE
SKILL: NO SKILL
LIKE: BROTHER

.hack// LEGEND OF THE TWILIGHT

MAHO   NO DATA

RUMOR

JOB: ??
SEX: ??
SKILL: ??
LIKE: ??

Rumor

NO DATA   NO DATA

.: 1 :.

Behind my FMD, I slammed my fist against the desk. "Why won't you use the reviving spell command?"

Lava oozed everywhere in the dungeon. Brigit, my blade-using avatar, was a gray ghost on the screen. She was dead. She wasn't the only one. My friend Maho also died in battle, and now our third party member, a Twin User, was being an ass.

"You agreed to revive us if we died down here!" Even though we were dead, we could communicate to our other party members.

"But you have a Wavemaster," the Twin User enthusiastically pointed out.

"Maho can't revive anyone once she's *dead*, so I'm asking you! You brought us here in the first place, because you said you were familiar with the area and we could gain a lot of experience points. It's your fault we're dead!"

The Twin User shrugged nonchalantly.

I lost it. "Dumb ass! We're a party, so you need to take care of your comrades! The Wavemaster isn't just a tool for you to recover your hit points. You need to protect us; we work as a team. Besides, as a Twin User, aren't you supposed to be multi-talented?"

"Sorry, I've gotta go."

"What?"

"I'm dropping out." The avatar entered a luminous circle to log out. "I didn't want to say this, but you guys suck."

"That jerk! How could he abandon us like that?!" I ranted, half-mad at myself for allowing us to join such a greedy, selfish player.

"Forget it. He's gone," Maho said.

"But I've never heard of an insensitive Twin User! He could've at least revived us before he left!"

"I'm sorry I got you into this mess."

"It's not your fault, Maho. That guy was ridiculous. Some hero, huh?"

Anytime a player didn't get their way, or abandoned their comrades, they were sarcastically called a hero.

"Damn, I wish we had waited for my brother instead of gaming with that idiot." I watched as the monsters that killed us walked past our corpses.

"What do you want to do now?" I asked. "Do you want to continue, just the two of us? Or should we return to the root town and find someone better?"

"Umm, well, I'm actually thinking of quitting The World," Maho said.

"What? Why?" I paused. "I mean, it's not your fault, Maho."

"No, it's not that."

"Then what? Is something wrong?" I asked.

"I'm just getting tired of it," she replied.

"Whaaat?"

"Online games don't really have a story. There aren't really any final authorities. It never ends and there's no objective, right? So basically, all you can do is beat up monsters and become stronger."

"Yeah, I guess. But that's how online games are." I shrugged.

"But you can't become a true hero, you know."

"What do you mean?"

"Well, since I can't be a hero in real life, I wanted to be one in the game world."

"If we keep killing monsters, we can increase our levels. Maybe we can try to be heroes," I suggested lamely.

"No matter how long we played or how hard we tried, we would never catch up to people who've been playing for years," Maho said.

She had a point.

"I like RPGs, but accumulating experience points is so boring! The painful part is seeing your comrades die, you know? I'm . . . I'm sensitive to that."

"So you think The World is boring?"

"I just don't think it's for me. Why waste time developing a character after paying the fee, blowing my days off, getting stressed, and then losing my character when data is lost? It's pointless."

"So, you're really quitting?" I asked.

"I thought I'd let you know, since we've gamed for so long. Thanks."

"If you want to play again, please e-mail me!"

"Okay."

Maho logged out. I haven't heard from her since.

.: 2 :.

I was alone when three giant caterpillar creatures ambushed me. I knew it would be hard to play solo, but I didn't realize *how* hard it could be.

I defended with my shield and swung hard with my sword, inflicting a nasty wound on one of the monsters. Unfortunately, the third creature flanked me and scored a hit. I was paralyzed by the creature's venom.

Being alone, I had no comrades to help me recover from the toxin or defend me in my weakened state. I was as good as dead.

I almost threw the controller down, when a bright flash appeared. Spiritual energy formed into ice arrows that rained down on the creatures, killing them in one sweep.

It was the first time I'd ever seen a high-level summoning spell.

I turned to find who cast the spell command. Emerging from the trees was a high-level Wavemaster, wearing a colorful blue robe and carrying a staff of water-spirit summoning. It was a rare, high-level item. I shuddered, knowing I was in the presence of great power.

"Thank you." I bowed as soon as the feeling returned in my limbs.

"You're playing solo as a Blade User?" He spoke in a high-pitched boy's voice. As he came closer, I realized his avatar was merely a child. He removed his hood. His cherubic face reminded me of Cupid.

"If you're playing solo, make sure you have good equipment. Don't focus on attack or defense levels, think about status and spells."

"Is playing solo difficult?" I asked.

"It's best to join a party, but if you insist on playing solo, try being a Twin User or a Heavy Axe."

"I think Twin Users are overrated," I said angrily. "Of course I'm biased. Yesterday, I was burned by one."

I then told him what happened.

"The guy was a real hero, eh?"

"More like a real jerk."

"Once burned, twice shy?" the Wavemaster chuckled.

"I don't want to team up with anyone like that again. But I needed to join a party to raise my levels quickly."

He shook his head. "Character levels and player levels are two different things. Even if a character achieves a high level, a mediocre player will remain mediocre. No matter how many experience points you gain, you can't improve the level of your personality!"

"Have you met any high-level players like that?" I wondered, intrigued.

"Sure!" He smiled. "Once I help a player and become friends, I like to betray their trust and kill them." He pointed his staff at my avatar and targeted me. "The look on their faces is such a rush!"

I was speechless. He was a Player Killer!

"Just kidding!" He dropped his arms. "But there are players like that."

Suddenly, I didn't like him anymore, even if he did save my life.

I took a deep breath, searching for something safe to talk about. "What's the purpose of playing online games?"

"Purpose?"

"Why waste time growing a character and paying game fees, then losing hours of my life when there's no real ending or objective?"

"You seem like a smart kid." I wondered how he knew that I was a kid in real life. "It sounds like your friend couldn't find a purpose, so she left The World."

"Maybe the game ends when you get tired of it."

"There are two types of players in The World: those who like it, and those who don't. Eventually, both kinds quit, only those who don't like it quit a lot sooner than those who do."

"When did you start playing The World?"

"When it was born."

"You've been playing since the first release?" I gaped.

"That's one way of putting it."

"But you've never gotten tired of it after all these years?"

"Do you get tired of living? Of course not! In some ways, this is my life. That's why I never get bored."

He moved closer and asked, "Do you know about the dot-hackers?"

"Uh, I guess not," I responded, stupidly.

"Hidden somewhere in The World is a party destined to solve the final puzzle."

"The World has an ending?" I asked, surprised.

"Of course, it could be just a rumor. It's dangerous to believe in online rumors. When you pass on a rumor to another player, you become an instigator. If you wish to pursue a rumor seriously, you need to develop a discerning ear for what's real and what's false."

I made Brigit nod and asked, "Are dot-hackers heroes?"

"In a fantasy RPG, a hero is someone who saves the world, right?" he asked.

"Sure. Everyone wants to be a hero."

"Then they'd want to be a dot-hacker."

"Who are dot-hackers? And how did they get that name?"

"The gossipers named them."

"So you don't know who they are?"

He smiled. "It's a fleeting rumor. The CC Corp. denies the existence of the Last Puzzle and there are no official statements regarding dot-hackers. They say they don't respond to any rumors. Period."

"So you could be making all this up?"

"Why would I do that? Besides, their response is perfectly logical. After all, if there were an end to the game, why would people pay money to play it afterward?"

I crossed my arms. "The World wouldn't survive if it really had an ending."

He brightened. "Maybe the Last Puzzle is a rumor CC Corp. started for publicity!"

"That's a possibility," I said.

The Wavemaster chuckled. "But I doubt it. The rumor wouldn't go away no matter how hard they tried to stop it. It just wouldn't disappear, and they tried real hard to make it go away."

"Where did you hear this rumor?"

"Rumors will always be vague. It's pointless to clarify rumors as they adjust and adapt to the time and place. But I heard there were two original members of the dot-hackers, Kite and Black Rose, a Twin User boy and a Heavy Blade girl."

"Who are you?" I asked.

"It's a rumor, after all. You don't have a discerning ear yet." The Wavemaster of water-spirit summoning looked at me. "But, now, this information, like a ripple on a calm surface, will enhance you. What you do with those feelings is up to you. Only you can decide. I might know more about The World than you do now, but I don't know your future. I can only follow events after the fact. You have to choose your own future."

He then turned his back on me and walked away.

Later, I checked his name on the chat log. When I looked it up in the Japanese-English dictionary, I found out his name meant *rumor.*

.: 3 :.

"Meow! So that's what your old character looked like, Rena? Wow!" I had met two new players, Mireille, the Wavemaster, and Orca, a werewolf. After telling them how my old character died, they wanted to take a look at the previous avatar, so I showed them Brigit's shadow.

Mireille hovered around Brigit, full of curiosity.

"You looked so different back then!" She giggled.

Mireille's avatar resembled a buff female knight wearing plate armor, with long, gray hair reaching down to her ankles, and an imprint of the fire Wave on her body.

"Different?" I asked, looking at Brigit. "In what way?"

"More rigid," Mireille answered.

"Aggressive," said Orca.

They didn't pull any punches. "You don't have to be so blunt!"

"Meow! Rena is mad!"

"Hey, we're not talking about you in real life."

It saddened me to know Brigit was dead. That's why I had to create my new avatar, Rena.

"Hey, while we're waiting for my brother, let me ask you something."

"What?"

"Why do you guys play in The World?" I asked.

"To find rare items," Mireille answered, nodding.

"To test my strength," said Orca.

"What about you, Rena?" Mireille looked at me with her large, starry eyes.

"Rena wants to make Shugo a hero," Orca laughed.

Beyond my FMD speakers, I heard the sound of someone opening the front door.

"Hold on, my brother's finally home!"

I pulled off my FMD and heard Shugo's footsteps approaching. "Hurry up," I screamed at Shugo. Then, into the microphone said, "Okay, we're almost ready to go on an adventure."

"We found a low-level area well suited for your brother so he can gain experience points," Orca said.

"Shugo, you're late! Everyone's been waiting for you! I'm going to log back in as Rena, okay?"

I logged Brigit out. Rena and Shugo logged in together and we played as a real team. I had found my one true hero sitting next to me.

Firefly

FAIRY
JOB: ??
SEX: ??
SKILL: QUIZ
LIKE: ??

.hack// LEGEND OF THE TWILIGHT

SANJURO
SUNAARASHI

NO DATA

FIREFLY??
JOB: WAVEMASTER
SEX: ??
SKILL: BEGINNER
LIKE: BOSTON CELTICS

Firefly

NO DATA   NO DATA

.: 1 :.

Boston is a town full of history; a history that included my dad's favorite team, the Boston Celtics. Dad grew up watching them during the 80s, at their height of excellence, when Larry Bird was their star player. Before 1986, they won sixteen national championships. Thirty years later, and they've never even come close to winning another.

My parents were an interesting couple. My dad, in typical Bostonian fashion, was a red-haired, hard-drinking Irishman. But as much as he loved sports and drink, he also enjoyed the arts. That's how he met my mom.

Mom was born in Kyoto, Japan. She came to the states to study and fell in love with my dad when they met at an art museum. She said it was love at first sight.

After many years of marriage, they still had their occasional squabbles. Tonight was one of those times. Mom had tickets to go to the opera on the same night as the NBA playoffs.

I guess Dad agreed to go because he didn't think the Celtics would make it this far. No one did. But the team somehow pulled off a miracle, and tonight was the final game in the series.

Although they'd argued about the game all week, in the end, my father's love for my mom outweighed his love of the sport. He made me promise to record it and not say a word about who won when he came home. It was an easy promise to make. I had no intention of watching the game.

Once I knew they were gone, I ran into my room and turned on my computer. I was going on a trip. I donned my FMD and clicked on ALTIMIT OS.

I knew my dad would be angry if he found out that I not only skipped dinner and the opera to play an online game, but also missed taping the playoff game that he so desperately wanted to stay home and watch. But I was fairly devious when it came to exploiting the family rules.

I tapped the keyboard and entered a world without borders. I wanted to go to my mom's country. I was going to Japan.

.: 2 :.

I stood on the streets of the river city, Mac • Anu. Beautifully strange and colorful flags waved along the canal. The city resembled an old European town, almost like Boston, but medieval. Best of all, my ears were full with the sounds of the very language I had come to hear: Japanese.

Growing up in Boston, I felt right at home with my Irish heritage, but my Japanese roots always seemed so distant. I wanted to learn Mom's language. Unfortunately, a trip to Japan was too expensive. So I did the next best thing. I set up an account on the Japanese server of the world's largest online game, The World.

Of course, my mom taught me some Japanese, and I took a couple college courses, but I wanted the opportunity to *really* test myself.

Looking around Mac • Anu, I noticed I was surrounded by players carrying swords, spears, staffs, and all of them were speaking Japanese. I listened to conversations as they passed by, then decided to wander the streets. As I peered into shops, I realized I had to be careful of what I bought, since I didn't understand everything.

After wandering around town awhile, I began to get bored and wanted to go on an adventure. Only I couldn't figure out how to leave. I wandered back and forth, but couldn't find any gates or exits. I was trapped in Mac • Anu.

I had wandered down an alley, when I decided to try out my linguistic skills on a pair of passing characters.

"Excuse me," I asked the one carrying an axe.

"Yes?"

I wanted to ask how to leave town, but everything I said came out garbled.

"What's that?" asked the Heavy Axe.

His partner, a female Wavemaster, turned and said, "He's probably a *gaijin*."

She continued speaking, but I had trouble following what she said, since she spoke so quickly. At any rate, I knew what *gaijin* meant. It was slang for *foreigner*. Even if my avatar looked Japanese, my broken Japanese quickly revealed I was not a native speaker.

"Let's go! We don't have time for this," the Wavemaster said, as they turned and quickly walked away.

Thus far, my cultural interaction wasn't going all that well.

I needed to understand the basics of The World before interacting with others. I was about to take off my FMD to review the player's manual, when I heard a giggle.

I looked around, but couldn't find anyone. I thought I was alone in the alley.

"Hello!" someone whispered in my ear.

A faint light appeared above me and slowly floated closer. It was a small, glowing fairy that could fit in the palm of my hand.

"What is the one thing there are not two of in The World?" it asked.

.: 3 :.

"What is the one thing there are not two of in The World?" it repeated, its wings fluttering.

I concluded that this was a game event. I looked back at the Japanese text. Rereading the riddle, I realized it was asking me to name something unique in The World. Unfortunately, I'd only been playing for five minutes. How would I know?

The fairy giggled and posed the riddle again.

"I don't know," I answered in my best Japanese.

It kept circling through the air and repeating the riddle. Finally, I ran away.

I pushed my way through a mob of characters onto the crowded street and ran across the bridge that arched over the canal. I stopped at the top of the arch and turned to see the fairy right before my eyes. It circled my head and continued giggling, repeating its riddle, "What is the one thing there are not two of in The World?"

"Please help me!" I pleaded in English, but everyone ignored me.

I felt helpless. This game was just too much.

"What's wrong? Are you in trouble?" someone asked in English. I must have been muttering aloud for someone to actually take notice.

I turned and saw a character standing at the foot of the bridge holding a samurai sword. I recognized his class as a Heavy Blade. His character wore an eye patch.

"I can help you if you want," he continued in English.

"You understand me?"

"Of course. I'm American." He laughed.

"Really? Me, too!"

"My name is Sanjuro Sunaarashi."

I introduced myself and then he asked, "Are you logged in from the U.S.?"

"Yes! Boston."

"Great town." He smiled.

"Do you live there too?"

"No. But I visited a long time ago. The lobsters were delicious. We don't get too many fresh lobsters in South Dakota. You know, where Mount Rushmore is located."

"Oh yeah, where the presidents' faces are carved in the mountain!" I laughed.

It's fascinating how people bond over their commonalities when traveling, even if we were only tourists on the net. Already, I was warming up to Sanjuro.

"So what's the problem?" he asked.

I told him everything that had happened since I first logged in.

Sanjuro nodded as he listened. Then he asked, "Is the fairy still here? Can you see it?"

I was confused since the fairy was flittering around me the whole time we talked.

"Can't you see it? It's right in front of me." I said.

"Hm . . . Let's go somewhere that isn't so noisy," Sanjuro suggested.

Since our chat could be heard by other people crossing the bridge, we moved down to the riverbed.

"You can't see this, Sanjuro?" I asked, surprised.

"No. I can't."

"But it's here! I'm pointing at it!"

"I believe you. It's probably a special event that only you can see." Sanjuro sat down on the riverbed. I didn't know the command for sitting down, so I remained standing.

"Only I can see it? How is that possible?" I watched the fairy flutter about, enraptured.

"This is an online game, so things are different from the real world. I don't doubt your story. Legends say that only innocent children can see fairies anyway!"

As he looked at a gondola drifting by, Sanjuro laughed out loud.

"I'm thirteen," I said. "Fairies wouldn't come to me at my age."

"Thirteen?! Is your voice altered?"

I heard that you could alter your voice using specific software. In cyberspace, you could change your voice, your age, your body type, or even your gender. The thick, manly voice of the samurai could actually be coming out of a cheerleader or a polite business executive. You never knew whom you were really dealing with.

"You said the fairy posed a riddle, right?"

"Yes."

"I've never heard of an event like that before." Sanjuro thought for a moment, then asked, "What did the fairy say to you?"

I went back to my chat log and repeated the riddle in Japanese.

He sighed and pondered aloud, "I wonder if it's referring to the gaming World? 'One thing that isn't two' means it's something unique."

"Do you have a guess?"

"Maybe it's a limited special event or a unique monster such as The One Sin?"

"The One Sin?"

"A pair of characters known as the Descendents of Fianna defeated a unique monster that could only be fought and beaten once."

"I'll try that answer."

I typed in The One Sin in *katakana*.

"No, no," the fairy giggled and shook its head.

"That wasn't it."

"I see. Ask if there are any hints?" Sanjuro said.

"Little fairy, I would like a hint," I said in Japanese.

"Hint, hint! The hint is that everyone has it!" The fairy somersaulted through the air leaving a trail of glitter in its wake.

I was even more confused. If it was one of a kind, how could everyone have it?

"What did it say?"

"The hint is that everyone has it."

I opened and scanned through my item list. However, as a newbie to the game, I couldn't possibly have something unique.

"An item in The World that everyone has, but there aren't two of, huh?"

"Isn't it weird? How can everyone own something unique?"

Sanjuro suddenly laughed. "You don't need to answer it now. The fairy will probably follow you as you continue the game, so let's go."

"What?"

"Let's go out in the field. You've never been out before, right?" He didn't wait for a response and then led me away.

After crossing the bridge, we reached an open area where a large mirror-like circle spun around and around. It was in the same place I started when I logged in.

"This is a Chaos Gate. It transports you anywhere in The World. You can go from a town to another area, or to other servers," he explained. "You can pick an area to go to by choosing a combination of three keywords."

I opened the Chaos Gate menu.

"Try choosing these three keywords." Sanjuro suggested a location and the Chaos Gate reacted, swallowing my avatar in a ring of light.

.: 4 :.

I stood in a grassy field. It was night. I could see the moon and the stars light up the sky. The wind swept across the plains, and I could hear the grass rustling. Only one thing was missing.

"Sanjuro?"

The samurai was nowhere to be seen. The giggling fairy was my only company.

"Where are you? Sanjuro?"

I stepped through the tall grass. In contrast to the noise and activity of the root town, the grassy field was silent, except for the faint sound of flowing water. I ran toward the water, the fairy following close behind.

I stopped when I heard something hit the water. I had stepped into a small creek. Then I heard another sound. As I scanned the area, I witnessed strange shadows moving on the other side of the water. It couldn't be Sanjuro.

The voices became louder as I moved upstream. I could hear several people talking about something.

Suddenly, a flash of lightning hit one of the characters.

Before I knew what had happened, I ran to the fallen player. It was the large Heavy Axe that I met in the back alley of Mac • Anu—the one that had walked away from me. He was dead.

The Wavemaster gulped at the sight of her partner's corpse. Then three characters emerged from the darkness to surround her.

Two were scraggly Heavy Blades holding samurai swords. The third was a Twin User resembling a ninja.

"So, there was a third one, huh." The long-haired Heavy Blade who killed the Heavy Axe glared at me. The other two laughed. It ticked me off.

"Are you guys PKs?" the Wavemaster shouted.

PK? What was a PK?

"Yep. And you're our prey." The long-haired Heavy Blade snickered. He was waving his sword back and forth between me and the Wavemaster, apparently trying to decide who would be next.

"Why?" I asked. "Why did you kill him?"

"What the hell? Is he a *gaijin?*" The long-haired Heavy Blade looked at me funny.

"How could you kill people?!"

"Stop speaking English, stupid! This is a JP server!" The long-haired Heavy Blade bellowed and pointed his sword at me. I had a feeling I would be next.

"Die!" he shouted.

I closed my eyes as the glinting sword swung downward. I heard the swoosh, but when I opened my eyes, Sanjuro stood before me.

"Sorry I'm late."

He struck the long-haired Heavy Blade with his sword and the rogue staggered from the forceful blow. All the three outlaws stepped back.

"Who the hell are you?"

"Do you wish to continue this battle?" Sanjuro spoke in Japanese.

The Heavy Blade turned to his companions. "He's too strong."

"What?"

"His level is too high!"

How did he know that? Could he tell just from the amount of damage he received?

The long-haired Heavy Blade was ready to flee and that seemed to dampen the spirits of the other two.

Sanjuro sensed their hesitation and barked a simple command, "Leave."

They fled like dogs.

"Filthy PKs are just like *ronin* . . . They have no pride or honor." Sanjuro remarked as he put away his sword.

"What's a PK?"

"A Player Killer," he explained.

"Why do they do that? Are they allowed to kill other people?"

Sanjuro didn't answer.

If the rules of The World allowed it, then I guess it was acceptable. But I couldn't understand why anyone would want to do that. The image I had of The World, and everything I had hoped to find in it, crumbled.

"Do those people play just to hurt others?"

"There are those that log in for that kind of stimulation," Sanjuro said.

"I just wanted to practice my Japanese. But if The World is like this, I don't want to play anymore."

The female Wavemaster politely bowed to me. "Thank you for saving us."

As she turned and thanked Sanjuro, I noticed the Heavy Axe was alive again.

"Thanks!" He looked happy as he spoke to me.

"How did you come back to life?"

"She resurrected me." He chuckled. Then his demeanor changed and he asked, "We met you back at town, didn't we?"

"Yes."

"I feel bad for ignoring you back there. I'm sorry."

The Heavy Axe introduced himself as Tamotsu, and she was Aki. The two of them were married in real life. Then I heard the sound of insects.

"Hey! It's almost time," Aki said.

"Almost time for what?" I asked.

"You'll see soon enough." Tamotsu pointed toward a soft glow of light. Slowly, the glow multiplied; first one, then two, then another and another. The tiny orbs appeared over the river, ever increasing in numbers.

"Fireflies!" I said.

"They're so pretty," said Aki. "We logged in to see them."

"But we didn't expect to run into PKs. I suppose you bump into a lot of things in The World." Tamotsu grinned.

"I remember when I was little I saw fireflies at the small creek near my grandmother and grandfather's house. That's my only memory of Japan."

"You've been to Japan?" asked Sanjuro.

"My mom is Japanese." And then it hit me. "I know the answer to the riddle."

I looked at the fairy and typed in the answer.

"Correct! Correct!" The fairy somersaulted gleefully.

"What is the answer?" asked Sanjuro.

"The one thing everyone has and yet there are no two of in the world is—your name!"

"How did you figure it out?"

"You can't register a name that already exists. When I first tried to register my name, I tried 'Hotaru' in *hiragana*, but it was already being used. I also tried it in *katakana* and *kanji*, but they were also taken. That's why I used English letters for my name, Hotaru, which means firefly."

The fairy frolicked in the air, then turned into a large ball of light and joined the fireflies. A moment later, the fireflies scattered into the night sky. Only the sound of the softly flowing river remained.

"Sanjuro, did you already know the answer?" I asked.

He smiled. "Why do you ask?"

"Because you brought me here to see my namesake."

Sanjuro chuckled.

"Well, we're going back to town," Tamotsu said.

"Thank you for saving us, Sanjuro Sunaarashi. Thank you, Hotaru." Aki waved.

They smiled and transported out in a ring of light. It fell quiet.

"You're getting better at your Japanese, kiddo."

"Huh?"

"You were speaking to those two in Japanese for quite awhile."

I suddenly realized he was right. I managed an entire conversation without speaking English.

"Here," Sanjuro said, as a new window popped up on my screen.

"What is this?"

"It's my member address. That way you can contact me again in the future."

"Thank you very much!"

"Remember, when you're adventuring, you'll encounter good people and bad, just like you will in real life. Do your best to enjoy the game and be with those worthy of your time," Sanjuro said.

"I'm glad I met you!"

"Nice to meet you, too, Hotaru," Sanjuro said. "I hope your adventures, like your name, will be one of a kind."

● ⬡ ●

I logged out and removed my FMD. Somehow, my room looked different. I'd experienced a new world, one that existed only through satellite beams and fiber optic cables. In a mere heartbeat, I could visit Japan.

I wanted to log back in to meet more people right away, but it was getting late. My parents would be home soon. I went downstairs to eat my cold dinner and turned on the TV. The game had just ended; the Celtics lost by three points.

Afterword

This book is a collection of short stories mostly published in the *Monthly Comptique Extra Edition*.

"2nd Character" is the story of *AI buster* (the previous novel), but told from Hokuto's perspective and honing in on Haruka Mizuhara, the person behind the avatar.

"Wotan's Spear" is technically the sequel to the first book, taking place during the same time period as stories one through four of *.hack//Sign,* the anime. Please read the manga, *Legend of the Twilight, volume 3* with this story.

"Kamui" takes place almost four years after the Twilight Incident, and Kamui is now commander of the

Cobalt Knights. It was her turn to have an unnerving encounter with an AI.

"Rumor" was fairly easy to write. Rena, the little girl, had a complex personality, but I hope I was able to capture her properly. Rumor is a web poet and Vagrant AI who enjoys spreading rumors for his enjoyment.

In "Firefly," I tell the story of when Hotaru and Sanjuro first met.

Thus concludes my *.hack* assignment. I'd like to thank Tamura-sama, the Comptique editor and Kou Nanba-sama, the novel editor. Also, I look forward to working with Uchiyama-sama of Bandai and Matsuyama-sama of CyberConnect2 on the next project. Finally, I really appreciate the time I was able to work with Idumi-san no matter how brief it was.

I hope to see you all again in the future!

TOKYOPOP® SHOP

WWW.TOKYOPOP.COM/SHOP

Check out all the sizzling hot merchandise and your favorite manga at the shop!

HOT NEWS!

Check out the TOKYOPOP SHOP! The world's best collection of manga in English is now available online in one place!

BIZENGHAST POSTER

Bizenghast

PRINCESS AI POSTCARDS

Princess

I Luv Halloween Glow-in-the-Dark STICKERS!
I LUV HALLOWEEN

I LUV HALLOWEEN BUTTONS & STICKERS

WWW.TOKYOPOP.COM/SHOP

0 00000 00000 0

- LOOK FOR SPECIAL OFFERS
- PRE-ORDER UPCOMING RELEASES
- COMPLETE YOUR COLLECTIONS

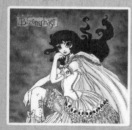

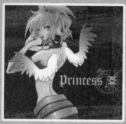

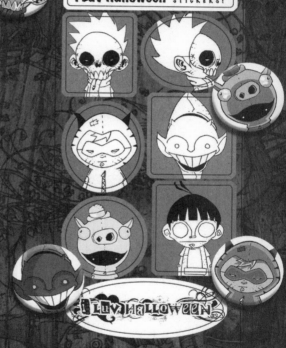

LIFE
BY KEIKO SUENOBU

Ordinary high school teenagers...
Except that they're not.

READ THE ENTIRE FIRST CHAPTER ONLINE FOR FREE:

Ayumu struggles with her studies, and the all-important high school entrance exams are approaching. Fortunately, she has help from her best bud Shii-chan, who is at the top of the class. But when the test results come back, the friends are surprised: Ayumu surpasses Shii-chan's scores and gets into the school of her choice—without Shii-chan! Losing her friend is so painful for Ayumu that she starts cutting herself to ease her sorrow. Finally, Ayumu seeks comfort in a new friend, Manami. But will Manami prove to be the friend that Ayumu truly needs? Or will Ayumu continue down a dark path?

Volume 1

LIFE

Keiko Suenobu

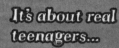

It's about real teenagers...

It's about real high school...

It's about real life.

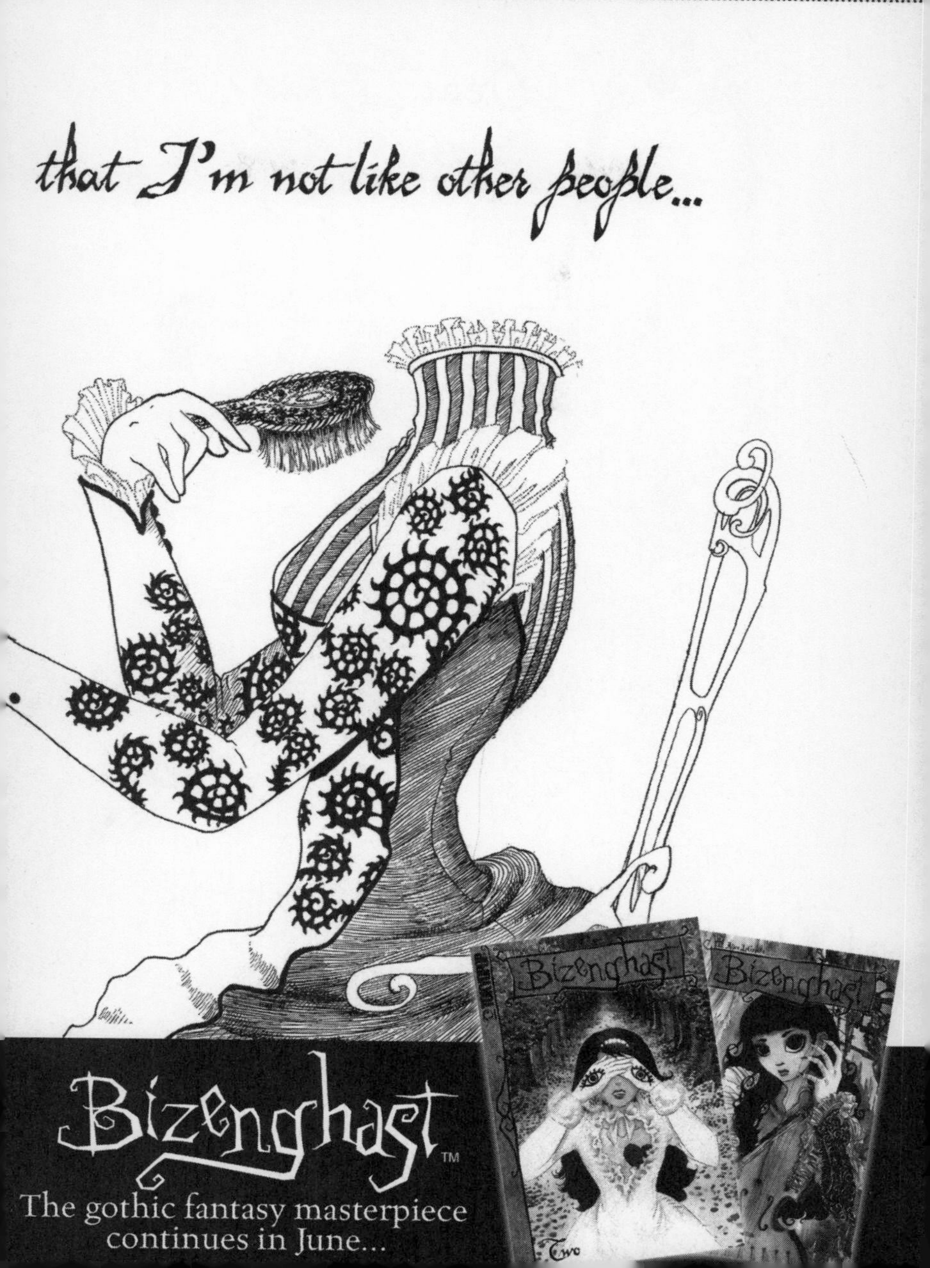
that I'm not like other people...
Bizenghast
Bizenghast
Bizenghast™
The gothic fantasy masterpiece
continues in June...

Music...mystery...and Murder!

RoadSong

Monty and Simon form the ultimate band on the run when they go on the lam to the seedy world of dive bars and broken-down dreams in the Midwest. There Monty and Simon must survive a walk on the wild side while trying to clear their names of a crime they did not commit! Will music save their mortal souls?

OT
OLDER TEEN
AGE 16+

READ A CHAPTER OF THE MANGA ONLINE FOR FREE:

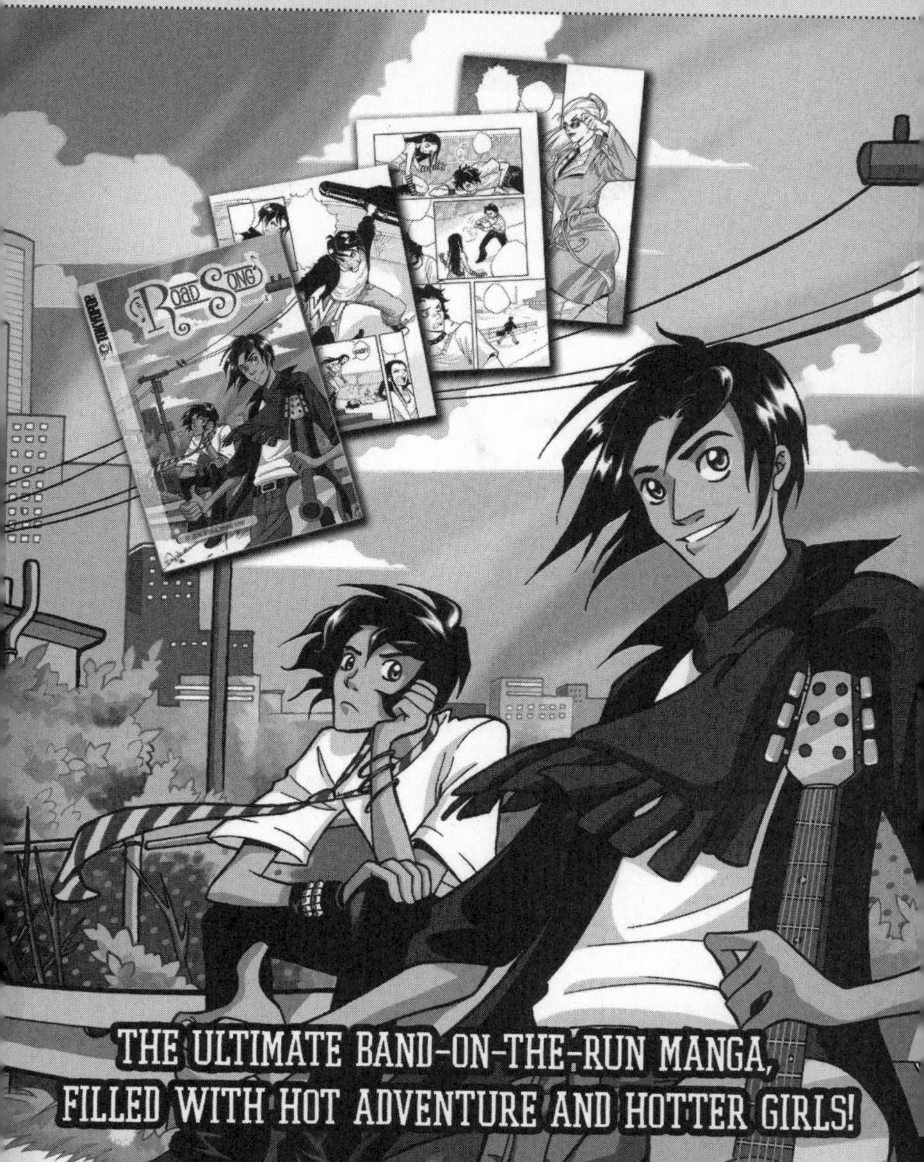
RoadSong
TOKYOPOP
THE ULTIMATE BAND-ON-THE-RUN MANGA,
FILLED WITH HOT ADVENTURE AND HOTTER GIRLS!

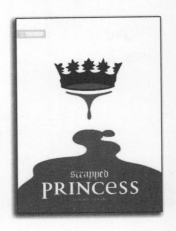

THIS FALL, TOKYOPOP CREATES A FRESH, NEW CHAPTER IN TEEN NOVELS...

For Adventurers...

Witches' Forest:
The Adventures of Duan Surk

By Mishio Fukazawa
Duan Surk is a 16-year-old Level 2 fighter who embarks on the quest of a lifetime—battling mythical creatures and outwitting evil sorceresses, all in an impossible rescue mission in the spooky Witches' Forest!

BASED ON THE FAMOUS
***FORTUNE QUEST* WORLD**

For Dreamers...

Magic Moon

By Wolfgang and Heike Hohlbein
Kim enters the enigmatic realm of Magic Moon, where he battles unthinkable monsters and fantastical creatures—in order to unravel the secret that keeps his sister locked in a coma.

THE WORLDWIDE BESTSELLING FANTASY
***THRILLOGY* ARRIVES IN THE U.S.!**

SPOTLIGHT

TOKYOPOP MANGA SUPPLEMENT

FRUITS BASKET

BY NATSUKI TAKAYA

Fruits Basket™

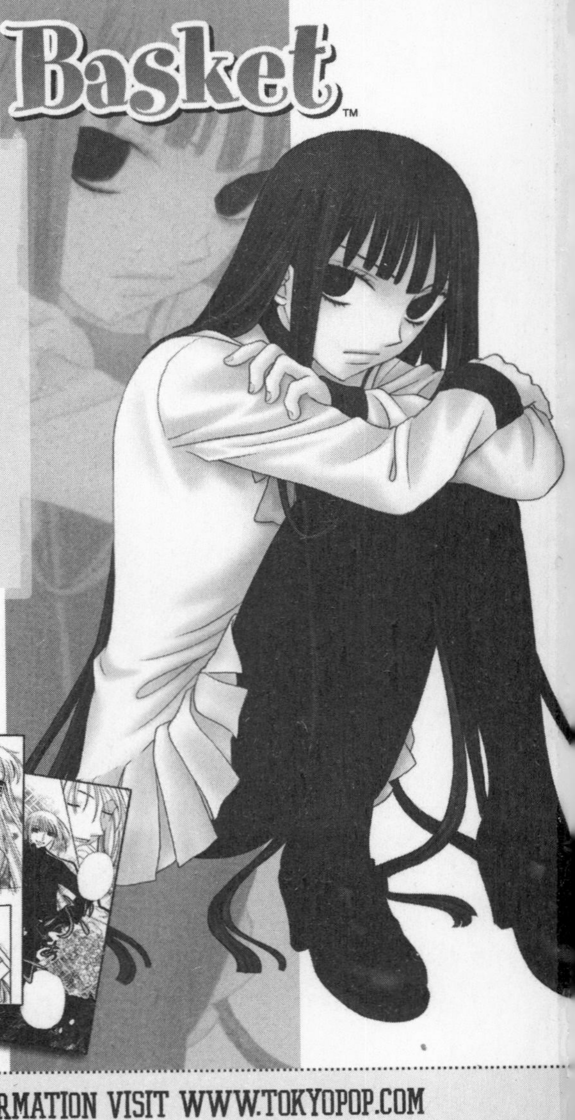

Tohru Honda was an orphan with no place to go...until the mysterious Sohma family offers her a place to call home. Tohru's ordinary high school life is turned upside down when she's introduced to the Sohmas' world of magical curses and family intrigue. Discover for yourself the Secret of the Zodiac, and find out why *Fruits Basket* has won the hearts of readers the world over!

THE BESTSELLING MANGA IN THE U.S.!

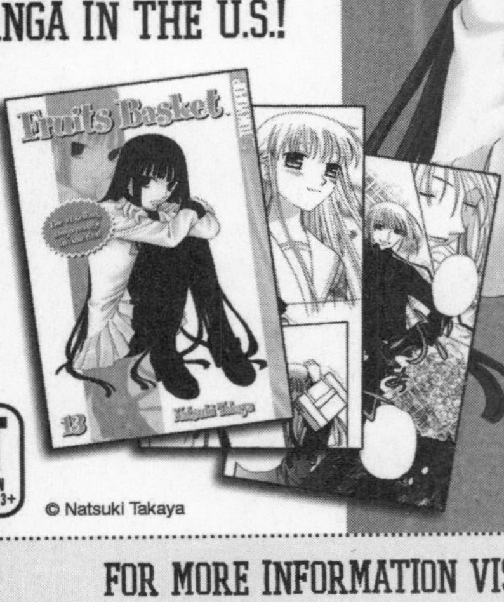
Fruits Basket
13

T
TEEN
AGE 13+

© Natsuki Takaya

FOR MORE INFORMATION VISIT WWW.TOKYOPOP.COM